May God encoura[ge] ♥ [you]
through this book
♥ Helen

Plant a Geranium in your Cranium

Other Books by Barbara Johnson

Where Does a Mother Go to Resign?

Fresh Elastic for Stretched-Out Moms

Stick a Geranium in Your Hat and Be Happy!

Splashes of Joy in the Cesspools of Life

*Pack Up Your Gloomees in a Great Big Box,
Then Sit on the Lid and Laugh!*

Mama, Get the Hammer! There's a Fly on Papa's Head!

I'm So Glad You Told Me What I Didn't Wanna Hear

Living Somewhere Between Estrogen and Death

Boomerang Joy

He's Gonna Toot and I'm Gonna Scoot

Leaking Laffs Between Pampers and Depends

Daily Splashes of Joy

God's Most Precious Jewels Are Crystallized Tears

BARBARA JOHNSON

Sprouting Seeds of Joy in the Manure of Life

THOMAS NELSON
Since 1798

NASHVILLE   DALLAS   MEXICO CITY   RIO DE JANEIRO   BEIJING

Published in Nashville, Tennessee, by Thomas Nelson. Thomas Nelson is a registered trademark of Thomas Nelson, Inc.

Thomas Nelson, Inc. books may be purchased in bulk for educational, business, fund-raising, or sales promotional use. For information, please e-mail SpecialMarkets@ThomasNelson.com.

Unless otherwise indicated, Scripture quotations used in this book are from the Holy Bible, New International Version (NIV). Copyright © 1973, 1978, 1984 International Bible Society. Used by permission of Zondervan Bible Publishers. Other Scripture references are from the following sources:

The King James Version of the Bible (KJV).

The Living Bible (TLB), copyright © 1971 by Tyndale House Publishers, Wheaton, Illinois. Used by permission.

The Message (MSG) © 1994 by Eugene H. Peterson and published by NavPress, Colorado Springs, CO 80935. Used by permission.

The Holy Bible, New Century Version (NCV), copyright © 1987, 1988, 1991 by W Publishing Group, Nashville, Tennessee 37214. Used by permission.

The chapter-ending collections of quips and jokes have been contributed by the author's many friends, and we have diligently tried to identify the material's origin. Where no source is named, the writer is unknown, and the author claims no rights or ownership.

The poem "Afraid? Of What?" by E. H. Hamilton is reproduced from Mrs. Howard Taylor's book, *John and Betty Stam: A Story of Triumph* (Overseas Missionary Fellowship, 1982). It is used here with permission of OMF International.

"The Servant Song" by Richard Gillard © 1977 Scripture in Song (a div. of Integrity Music, Inc.)/ASCAP c/o Integrity Music, Inc., 1000 Cody Road, Mobile, AL 36695. Used with permission of Integrity Music, Inc.

ISBN 978-0-8499-3785-9

Printed in the United States of America

07 08 09 10 11   QW   14 13 12 11 10

Contents

Unexpected foresight . . .

Shopping at the mall near my home in early February 2001, I met a friend I hadn't seen in a long time.

"Oh, Barb, you look great. You've lost weight, haven't you?" she gushed.

"No, I just got my hair cut," I answered, a little embarrassed because I hadn't lost a single pound.

"Well, then, you ought to get your entire head shaved, because you really look fabulous," she replied.

Little did I know . . .

I don't know what the problem is . . . but I'm sure it's hard to pronounce

Where are we going, and why am I in this handbasket?

What a luxury it was to have a few days at home in the middle of March 2001, with no traveling, no speaking engagements, no out-of-town guests to entertain. Women of Faith had just commenced its 2001 tour a couple of weeks earlier in Charleston, West Virginia, and Bill and I had enjoyed being back on the road with our traveling companions of the last five years. But now it was good to be home again with a few days to get caught up on all the work before the tour shifted into high gear. In the next eight months Women of Faith would be presenting conferences in twenty-five cities from coast to coast, including one stretch of seven back-to-back weekends without a break. It was going to be an exciting, *exhausting* year.

To celebrate my "downtime" I was puttering around the house, tending to little chores we hadn't had time to do for several months. For example, I'd noticed that my clothes dryer wasn't drying clothes as fast as it once had. Someone told me it helped the dryer run more efficiently if you cleaned out all the lint that had collected not just in the lint trap but underneath the trap, too, in all the reachable corners of the dryer's outer shell. So, while Bill was out running errands, I armed myself with an old toothbrush and settled onto the floor in front of the dryer to dig out all the fuzz that had accumulated.

I was happily excavating long strings of lint when the strangest feeling came over me. Suddenly, my arms and legs became as flimsy as wet noodles. There was no pain, no tingling, no dizziness. Just an overwhelming sense of weakness. I felt fine—except that I just couldn't get up. I oozed onto the floor—and stayed there. Suddenly I regretted all the times I'd made fun of that old lady in the TV commercial for the health-monitoring device—the poor old thing who pushed the button on her radio pendant and shouted, "Help! I've fallen and I can't get up!"

No Time for Trouble
There was no pain, no nausea, no discomfort at all. I just couldn't muster the strength to get up off the floor. It was the strangest sensation I've ever known.

Eventually Bill came home. It really irked me that, seeing me sprawled on the laundry-room floor, he didn't immediately sense that something was wrong. "I thought you just got carried away with your toothbrush and decided to clean *under* the dryer, too," he said later.

He helped me get up and into a chair, and we discussed whether we should call my doctor. But it seemed so silly to call up and say, "I feel fine, except that my arms and legs have suddenly turned into stretched-out rubber bands." I thought my doctor, who had known me for years and read all my books, might tease me. "Well, what do you need, Barb," I imagined him saying, "fresh elastic?"

Throughout the afternoon friends called to say hello. When I told them the perplexing and rather unusual thing that had happened, they didn't think it was funny at all. Every one of them fussed and threatened to call 911 long distance and send the medics hurrying to my rescue. They worried that I'd had a stroke. But I laughed and reassured them. I knew I hadn't had a stroke. I could talk and think and function the same as always. I had just been unable to get up off the floor.

"I'm fine," I told them all.

But it was obvious there would be no peace until I had myself checked out. In fact, I began worrying that some of my fussbudget friends might have a stroke themselves, worrying about me, if they didn't calm down. So the next morning, feeling sure I was wasting my time, I drove myself to my doctor's office. And the next thing I knew, I was checked into a hospital, assigned to a different doctor—a specialist in neurology—and was being poked and prodded and scanned until I absolutely had no secrets left from anyone!

ZIGGY   By Tom Wilson

The tests went on for a couple of days. Then the next morning the neurosurgeon came into my room, trying to look pleasant but obviously hiding some hard news.

"Well, Mrs. Johnson," he said kindly. "We think we've narrowed down the problem to two possibilities."

"Oh . . . that's good—I guess," I said, not sure how to respond. "What are my choices?"

He laughed. "Well, it's not really a choice. And neither one is something you'd ever *choose*. It looks like you've either had a massive stroke . . . or you have a brain tumor."

"Ohhhh," I moaned. It took me a minute to catch my breath. Then I began pleading. "I don't have time for either one of *those* problems. I've got a ministry to run and twenty-five speaking engagements scheduled. We've got company coming this weekend, and we're leaving for Sacramento next Thursday," I began, as though I could argue with him.

The doctor smiled nervously. "Mrs. Johnson, I wouldn't count on going to Sacramento if I were you . . ."

"So you think it's either a stroke or a brain tumor . . ." I was barely able to repeat his devastating words. I had to let them soak into my poor, besieged brain until finally I could understand what he was telling me. "Which one should I pray for? It's like choosing between Hitler and Mussolini!"

He laughed. "No, it's not the greatest choice, is it? But I think we should pray it's a tumor. Some brain tumors are very treatable; a lot of them we can melt with chemotherapy. But the damage caused by a stroke is irreversible in many cases."

Obviously, I wanted to have the problem that could *melt* away. After all the harsh news the doctor had brought to me in those last few minutes, the word *melt* seemed soothing and peaceful.

He squeezed my hand and left the room.

A Major Change in Plans

An MRI would determine which condition was causing my problem. Now, MRI officially stands for Magnetic Resonance Imaging; it's a high-tech test that lets doctors see horizontal "slices" of the inside of your body. But to me MRI stands for Mini-Roll Insertion or Magnificent Racket Inducer, because the experience made me feel like I was being inserted into the tiny center of a giant roll of bathroom tissue—or, more accurately, the even smaller metal tube of a toilet-tissue holder. Inside the tube, it sounded like a giant drummer was pounding away, right above my face.

Lying flat on my back on a slab, something like a conveyor belt slowly carried me into the tiny tube of the giant machine. The technician had cautioned me that it would be absolutely essential to lie perfectly still throughout the ninety-minute procedure—no coughing, scratching, shifting, twitching, or laughing—or the whole thing might have to be repeated. *Right!* I thought. *As if anyone could laugh when her head's disappearing into a giant steel toilet-tissue roll!* Then, as soon as I heard the lecture, I had the most urgent need to rub my nose. I gave it one good swipe as the conveyor belt started up then quickly tucked my hands by my sides, as instructed. It was a little scary, but fortunately, I'm not claustrophobic, so I wasn't overwhelmed by nervousness. Suddenly, I had the silliest image as I thought about what it was like to lie on that conveyor-belt bed. I thought about that *I Love Lucy* episode where Lucy's working in the chocolate factory and the conveyor belt brings the chocolates faster and faster until she's unable to keep up and starts shoving them into her mouth and down her blouse and under her hat. *Maybe I* will *laugh after all,* I mused. But just then the first *bong!* echoed through the tube, and I didn't have to worry about moving. For a moment, I was scared stiff!

After several minutes of the loud *bonging!* a voice seemed to come from right inside my head. "Mrs. Johnson? Are you all right? Are you doing okay?"

At first I thought it was God, calling me home. Then I realized it was the technician. (God would've called me "Barb.")

What I wanted to answer was, "Get me outta here! This is crazy! I feel like I'm stuck in a huge roll of aluminum foil!" Instead, I murmured, "Uh-huh. Just fine."

Finally, ninety minutes later, the test was over. Afterward, a friend sent me a clipping by Colorado humorist Chris Westcott, who wrote in the *Durango Herald* about her own MRI. She was the one who first compared the procedure to being put into a "vibrating metal canister roughly the size of the paper tube inside a roll of toilet paper." And she noted that before under-going the procedure, patients have to remove anything metal from their bodies since the scan uses a magnetic field. "The magnetic field didn't hurt," she said, "but when the scan was over, I did have a strange compulsion to walk due north."

"Relax, Mrs. Johnson. I'm just
going to give you a quick CAT scan."

Thank goodness I didn't feel the urge to head for the North Pole! But I did come out of the experience with a stronger urge to draw nearer to the Father. It started when a friend told me it helps, when you're having an MRI or CAT scan, to have someone hold your feet as you lie inside the tube. It reminds you you're not alone and provides comfort, she said.

Since that first one, I've had *lots* more MRIs and CAT scans, and several friends have volunteered to be my foot-holders, but I have declined. I've had Someone else helping me. When I'm in that small, confined space, I picture myself hidden away in "a cleft in the rock," covered gently with God's own hand as His magnificent glory thunders by, as Exodus 33:22 describes. And in that loud, tight, toilet-paper tube of a place, I feel an unusual sense of comforting peace.

Oh Good! It's a Tumor
Doctors should be required to take acting classes as part of their medical-school curriculum. Then when they have bad news to deliver they could be a little more successful in hiding their feelings as they approach the patient. My poor doctor walked in my room that day looking like a little boy who had been caught stuffing a frog down his sister's turtleneck.

"So far, the tests have ruled out anything inexpensive."

"Well, hello. Do you have news for me? It's okay," I told him, trying to be encouraging. "Whatever it is, God won't fall off His throne."

"It's a tumor," he said gently, "a little larger than a golf ball, deeply embedded in your brain. And we're almost certain it's cancer."

"Cancer . . . ," I echoed, frozen by that one awful, breathtaking word as though I'd been shot with a stun gun. It hung there over my hospital bed for a moment. Then it occurred to me: *This has to be a mistake! I can't have cancer. There's been no cancer in my family. I come from a long line of* heart-trouble *people. This guy obviously has me mixed up with someone else who landed on the laundry-room floor last week.*

"Cancer! It *can't* be cancer," I told the doctor emphatically. "My family doesn't get cancer. I'm supposed to die from a heart attack or a bad pulmonary valve or blocked artery. And I can't have a *brain* tumor. Why, I haven't even had a headache; how could I have a brain tumor?"

"We need to do surgery, a craniotomy," he continued, smiling indulgently at the shocked responses that poured out of me nonstop.

"A craniotomy! Brain surgery! How can this be? I feel fine, just a little weak, and I've got so much to do—those twenty-five Women of Faith conferences and book contracts and a ministry to run . . ." Wasn't this guy listening to me? Didn't he see I didn't have time for this? I COULD NOT HAVE A MALIGNANT BRAIN TUMOR!

"But we've got to reduce the swelling in your brain before we can operate," he rambled on as though I hadn't said a word. And maybe I hadn't. I was in such a state of shock, I wasn't sure what I was saying—or hearing. "We'll do that with medication," he said, "and then as soon as it's feasible, we'll do the surgery."

"I'm gonna have surgery? Brain surgery? You'll remove the . . . the tumor?" I asked, still unaccustomed to thinking the word had anything to do with *me*, with *my* head.

"Maybe," he answered. "We have to get a good look at it in order to know how best to treat it. If we can remove it without damaging healthy tissue, we'll do that. If not, we'll leave it alone and treat it with chemo. And of course we'll need to keep an eye on your diabetes while we're doing this."

Chemo. Another new word in the awful vocabulary that had suddenly been personalized for ME.

"Mrs. Johnson," he said, holding my hand, "I know this is hard news for you. And I suspect these next twenty-four hours, as you adjust to this news, will be the *hardest* twenty-four hours you've ever lived."

Somehow, his warning snapped me out of my shocked state. I looked at the doctor and actually smiled. *Doctor, I* thought, *you obviously know nothing about my life!*

Moments of Mirth in the Manure Pile

It's our tradition in my books to share a smattering of inspiring stories, funny jokes, and cartoons at the end of each chapter. They've all been sent to me from friends around the country, and in many cases the author is unknown. But obviously the writers were folks who loved to laugh. And oh, how we all need to laugh!

Probably the best-known sentiment about cancer, sent to me by a host of friends and well-wishers, is this little essay by an unknown writer:

> *Cancer is so limited.*
> *It cannot cripple love.*
> *It cannot shatter hope.*
> *It cannot corrode faith.*
> *It cannot eat away peace.*
> *It cannot destroy confidence.*
> *It cannot kill friendship.*
> *It cannot shut out memories.*
> *It cannot silence courage.*
> *It cannot invade the soul.*
> *It cannot reduce eternal life.*
> *It cannot quench the Spirit.*
> *It cannot lessen the power of the resurrection.*

A riddle:
Q: How do you make God laugh?
A: Tell Him your plans.

"Okay, for lunch you have a choice of liver, kidney, heart . . . oh, I'm sorry, this is your organ donor card."

The day the Lord created hope was probably the same day He created springtime.[1]

God loves to decorate. Let Him live long enough in a heart, and that heart will begin to change. God can no more leave a life unchanged than a mother can leave her child's tear untouched.[2]

If you want to be the *picture* of health, you're gonna need a happy *frame* of mind to put it in.[3]

Mixed maxims:
Don't count your chickens before they cross the road.
He who laughs first shall be last.
Beauty is only skin deep . . . in the eye of the beholder.[4]

Don't be a cloud
just because you failed to become a star.

Jesus didn't avoid storms—
He weathered them.
He didn't keep the boat out of the water—
He kept the water out of the boat![5]

My body is all messed up:
My nose runs, and my feet smell!

Errors have been made.
Others will be blamed.

The next best thing to *solving* a problem is
finding some humor in it.[6]

THE FAMILY CIRCUS   By Bil Keane

"We have these little dots on our chest so Doctor James knows where to put his microphone."

Love, joy, peace, patience, kindness, goodness,
*   faithfulness, gentleness, and self-control.*
To these I commit my day.
If I succeed, I will give thanks.
If I fail, I will seek his grace.
And then, when this day is done,
I will place my head on my pillow and rest.[7]

Energize the limp hands, strengthen the rubbery knees. Tell fearful souls, "Courage! Take heart! GOD is here." (Isaiah 35:3–4 MSG)

Having a tumor . . . with humor

It's been lovely, but I have to scream now

Looking back on the moments of the last year, I'm amazed at how suddenly my life screeched around what my friend David Jeremiah calls another "bend in the road." It's a steep, sharp-cornered road I know all too well.

My first experience with sudden life upheaval occurred as I literally rounded a bend in a mountain road and came upon a heap of a man lying on the pavement in a tangled mass of metal that had been his car. Only by his clothing could I recognize the mangled form as my husband, Bill, who had left home shortly before I had as we hauled two carloads of kids, luggage, and supplies to a mountaintop retreat.

Despite overwhelming odds, God healed Bill of his devastating injuries, and a couple of years later, on a beautiful, Southern California day, our lives suddenly shifted again from joy*ful* to joy*less* when a black military car slowly rolled to a stop in front of our house. Two marines in full-dress uniforms walked solemnly to our door, and even before I answered their knock, I knew what they would tell me: Our eighteen-year-old son, Steve, the second oldest of our four boys, had been killed in Vietnam.

Once again, we clung to God's lifeline of love as we slowly
emerged from the cesspool of sorrow and life returned to
almost normal. Then, five years later, Bill and I were presid-
ing over a boisterous family dinner with two of our sons
when the phone rang. And in less than sixty seconds, sorrow
once more enveloped us. Another son—our oldest, twenty-
three-year-old Tim—had been killed by a drunk driver.

So now we had two sons as deposits in heaven, and the
road of my life was starting to resemble a mountain road with
one hairpin curve after another. Then, a year after Tim died, I
hurried into our twenty-year-old son David's bedroom to
find a book for a friend who wanted to borrow it. As I opened
a drawer, I found magazines and letters that revealed to me
that David was homosexual. Later I confronted him with what
I'd found, saying many unloving things. As a result, he left
our home, disowned us, changed his name, and disappeared.
It would be eleven years before he came back into our lives
and our relationship was restored.

So many times, my heart has been broken and my world
has been turned upside down. And now a doctor was telling
me something in my brain the size of a *golf ball* was going to
be the hardest thing I'd ever had to endure? Not hardly!

In the midst of this ordeal, a friend sent me a poem written
many years ago by China missionary E. H. Hamilton in admiration of another missionary, J. W. Vinson, who was martyred in North China. It explains so beautifully the courage
Christians know when they're facing any sort of trial:

Afraid? Of What?

Afraid? Of what?
To feel the spirit's glad release?
To pass from pain to perfect peace,
The strife and strain of life to cease?
Afraid—of that?

Afraid? Of what?
Afraid to see the Savior's face,

To hear His welcome, and to trace
The glory gleam from wounds of grace?
Afraid—of that?

Afraid? Of what?
A flash, a crash, a pierced heart;
Darkness, light, oh heaven's art!
A wound of His a counterpart!
Afraid—of that?

Afraid? Of what?
To do by death what life could not—
Baptize with blood a stony plot,
'Til souls shall blossom from the spot?
Afraid—of what?[1]

Shock, Yes. Fear, No

As all parents know, it's much harder to deal with adversities affecting our children than it is to face something that hurts *us.* Let one of my loved ones suffer, and I'm beside myself with concern. And although it wasn't the easiest thing in the world to have a doctor stand over my hospital bed and tell me I had a malignant brain tumor, I never felt a moment of fear. Shock, yes. Sorrow, maybe. Fear, no.

Admittedly, *cancer* can be a terrifying word. It evokes images of no turning back, of having no control over your body and your life . . . not finishing the big game the way you wanted to. Hearing you have cancer can be one of the toughest challenges you will ever face.

Someone sent me a newspaper article about a well-known pastor who was diagnosed last year with a rare and aggressive form of cancer. The pastor admitted that when the doctor told him that cancer had invaded his body, his knees buckled.

Yes, I thought when I read that line, knowing exactly how that pastor felt, *our knees buckle. And that puts us in exactly the right position to ask God for help and to feel His hand resting on our lives.* The pastor, too, had felt shock but not fear. "I believe what I preach," he said. "I believe we're in the Lord's hands." The pastor had told his congregation, "Now you'll hear me preach with my life."[2] It's at times like these we need to remember this advice:

Don't forget in the dark
what you've learned in the light.

It's not that any of us would *choose* to have cancer. But as Christians we're in a win-win situation. Some wise wordsmith put it this way:

The *worst* that can happen is the *best* that can happen.

Christians know the truth of that statement. For surely the *worst* that can happen is that we die—and that's actually the *best* that can happen because we know we don't go from life to death. As singer Kathy Troccoli says so emphatically, when we die we go from life to *life*. We sigh out that last earthly breath and breathe in the glorious atmosphere of heaven!

Sprouting Geraniums
Just because I wasn't afraid to die, don't think for a minute that I had no qualms about what was going to happen to me up to that point! If the doctor had said, "You've got a brain tumor, and we're going to have to amputate your head," I could have lived with that—or died quickly and happily, flying off to heaven to get a whole new body. But of course that's not what he proposed. Instead, his treatment monologue was spattered with more words full of foreboding. Words like *surgery . . . several weeks of chemo . . . more tests*, and then that scariest of all phrases: *wait and see.*

The next thing I knew, my bedside seemed to have become a regular stop for a continually growing parade of physicians and other caregivers. My familiar endocrinologist who had helped me control my diabetes for years was joined by the neurosurgeon and an oncologist, an anesthesiologist, and an endless array of nurses, nurses aides, and lab and radiology technicians.

A couple of my friends were in the room when the surgeon came in and said he would be performing a craniotomy. He smiled encouragingly and with his finger drew a line from one ear, over the top of my head, to the other ear to show me where the incision would be made.

"I hope you know you'll be operating on a very special person, Doctor," one of my friends said while I grimaced and pursed my lips to say, *Shhhh!*

"Oh?" the doctor replied.

"Yes, this is the best-selling Christian female author of all time. Barbara has written more than a dozen best-selling books," the friend continued. The surgeon raised his eyebrows. "Is that so? What books did you write?"

"Her best-known books are *Stick a Geranium in Your Hat and Be Happy!* and *Living Somewhere Between Estrogen and Death,*" my motormouth friend went on. The doctor smiled politely as though he might have been thinking that of all the strange things he had heard about his patients, this was the strangest. He probably decided, *Obviously, this woman has needed brain surgery for a long, long time!*

"Actually, people get the *Geranium* title mixed up all the time," I told him. "One woman even asked me once if the title was *Stick a Geranium in Your Cranium.* I guess that will have to be my next book, now that I'm having a craniotomy."

The doctor smiled a little nervously, probably wondering if he should call in a psychiatrist for a consultation.

Prayers and Partying
Never known for my patience, if I had to have surgery I wanted to have it *now.* Today. This minute. Get it over with! But if you've ever been in a hospital, you know that the patient's desired timetable doesn't carry a high priority. The doctors said surgery would have to wait a few days until a course of steroids could reduce the swelling around the tumor. So all I could do was wait there in my hospital room—

and entertain visitors. A steady stream of family and friends flowed in and out of my tiny room as I grew increasingly irritated with each additional hour of waiting. How frustrating it was to think of all the work I needed to do at home and for Spatula Ministries and Women of Faith while I lounged on a hospital bed and spent day after day chitchatting mindlessly with an ever-changing assortment of faces as I waited for the swelling in my brain to go down!

Of course, there were moments of pure joy, even in that worrisome time. One morning about 5 A.M. I awakened to the strains of the music from *Little House on the Prairie*, one of my favorite TV shows. Wondering who would be up listening to that show so early, I realized someone was holding my hand, squeezing it lightly. In the soft light of the television screen, I made out the form of my big, 210-pound, six-foot-two son Barney standing there. What a shock—and what a delight—to see him beside my bed and to realize he had come to the hospital at that hour to watch my favorite show with me. When you're facing the unknown, it's such a comfort to find yourself holding a familiar hand and sharing a thoughtful experience.

Party Time

Finally, the night before the surgery was to be performed, several of my friends, including some of the other Women of Faith speakers, squeezed into my little room with Bill, our sons David and Barney, and Barney's wife, Shannon, for one last round of prayer and partying.

My friend and fellow Women of Faith speaker Sheila Walsh had endured her own adventures rushing to my bedside. When she arrived at the Orange County, California, airport, there were no rental cars available due to some kind of convention being held in the area. She didn't know how she would get all the way to St. Jude's Hospital, quite a distance away. Seeing the distraught look on her face as she slumped over the rental-agency desk, the man behind the counter asked her, "Do you *really* need a car?"

"Yes!" she answered emphatically.

"Well, stand right out there on the sidewalk, and a short guy in a red truck will come pick you up and take you to a rental car," the man said.

Not until she was actually seated beside the stranger in the red truck did Sheila have the tiniest bit of nervousness, probably remembering all the times she had told her son *never* to get in a car with a stranger! But the kind man delivered on his promise and took Sheila to another rental-car lot where she rented a car and drove to the hospital.

Inside the building, she somehow got on the wrong bank of elevators and ended up, without realizing it, in the maternity ward!

"Can you tell me where Barbara Johnson's room is?" Sheila asked a nurse.

"Of course," she replied. "Is it a boy or a girl?"

"Well, she's a girl, I guess, but she's in her seventies!"

The nurse looked at Sheila as if she were from the *Guinness Book of Records*. "I think you're in the wrong wing," she said. "I doubt that *that* Mrs. Johnson just had a baby!"

"Well, she's had four but . . . that's a long story. You should read her books!"

Finally, Sheila found my room, where she joined the ongoing party. At one point eighteen people were crowded into the little place. There was lots of laughter that night, but some trepidation, too. Then one of the gals suggested we sing.

Just as we got wound up and our voices were echoing down the tiled hallways, one of my monitors went off, beeping sharply above our impromptu concert. A nurse hurried into the room, saw the crowd, and apparently thought we were holding tryouts for a gospel choir.

"Oh, dear!" she said. "We can't have all these people in here. Mrs. Johnson needs to rest. We can't have this."

Are You Still There?

After another quick round of prayers, the party ended, and I was left alone to face the long, dark night. I lay there in the stillness, my face turned to the wall, and remembered a pastor's story I'd heard. He told about a little boy who awoke, frightened, in the night. The boy toddled off to find his parents and woke up his father with his mournful sobs.

The father returned to the son's bedroom with him and promised to lie down beside the boy's little bed until the child fell asleep again. They lay there in the darkness awhile and then the little boy whispered, "Daddy? I can't see you. Are you still there?"

"Yes, son, I'm here."

The boy lay still a moment, then the father heard his voice again.

"I can't see you, Daddy. Is your face turned toward me?"

"Yes, son, my face is turned toward you."

And that's what I wanted to know throughout that long night in the hospital. *Are You still there, God? Can You see me? Is Your face turned toward me?*

And the answer was the same one I had heard all my life: *Always!*

Reassured, I remembered again the beloved words of the ancient Aaronic blessing in Numbers 6:24–26:

> *The LORD bless you and keep you;*
> *the LORD make his face shine upon you*
>   *and be gracious to you;*
> *the LORD turn his face toward you and give you peace.*

Then, comforted once more, I whispered my own little two-word prayer, the same two words that have lifted me out of life's cesspool so many times before.

Whatever, Lord . . .

The Hardest Thing

After the sheep-shearer nurse did her thing the next morning, I looked like a cross between Groucho Marx and the Statue of Liberty. Everything from the back of my ears forward was shaved off—which made all the hair that was left look like wool sprouting out of a bowling ball. As Women of Faith president Mary Graham slipped into my room for the surgical send-off, her eyebrows shot up, and her mouth formed a big, round O. I could tell she wanted to cry—but didn't dare. So she laughed instead. "Barb, won't it be nice to have all new hair?" she asked enthusiastically, as though I were getting a new set of dishes or something. "I've heard it sometimes grows in *curly* after you shave it off."

"Yes, I've heard that, too," I said, gingerly touching my bald scalp. "But it sorta makes me feel bad about all those jokes I've told about men losing their hair. You know, I've said so many times that men don't lose their hair—it just goes underground and comes out their ears. I'll hate it if I have curly hair growing out of my *ears* when this is over."

After the sheep-shearer nurse did her thing, I looked
like a cross between Groucho Marx and the Statue of Liberty.

The surgery was scheduled for 11 A.M. But that time came and went with no sign of the surgical team. At noon, I was ready to march up to the operating room and bang on the door.

"Go call them," I told Mary Graham. "We need to go."

"It doesn't work that way, Barb," Mary answered. "It's not like calling a taxicab."

"Well, then, let's just go wait by the elevator, " I suggested to the friends and family who had reassembled in my room. "I want to get this over with!"

I eased out of bed, grabbed my IV pole, and headed for the elevator. The nurses had told me it would be good to do some walking before surgery, and I figured that was as good a place to walk to as any. My startled entourage had no choice but to follow. They settled into the lounge area where I instructed them to keep an eye on the elevator doors while my son David paced with my IV pole and me up and down the hall.

During a rest stop, the group invited me to sit down and sing with them again.

"Okay," I said, "let's sing 'I'll Fly Away.'"

"No!" Mary Graham blurted out. "Not that. It's not time for that. You're not gonna fly away *anywhere* today, Barb."

By one o'clock, two hours after the scheduled surgery time, we were still waiting by the elevator, and I'm sure my friends were thinking of asking if I might be moved into a room with padded walls and NO CLOCK, just in case I went completely berserk. Then, just before two, the elevator doors opened, and two transport aides wheeled out a gurney—my ride to the OR. I herded everyone back to my room and climbed up onto the cot. It was such a relief to finally be on my way to this dreaded ordeal, I was almost gleeful.

The group of friends trailed me back down the hallway as the orderlies wheeled me into the elevator. I'm sure the other patients on that floor must have thought I was either a criminal under heavy guard or a mental patient in danger of escaping, to have so many escorts following me all over the place!

To be honest, I don't remember a lot about that morning, but my loved ones have told me about it. Mary Graham shared these thoughtful memories of that time:

Barb, as we sat there that morning, you were so true to who you are. You had that same-as-always spirit and feistiness. It gave all of us an opportunity to see what you were like under intense pressure, and you were exactly like you always are. I'll never get over that. When they wheeled you away, you were still talking to us, reassuring us. It was as if you were just going down the hall to get your shoes shined. You told me, "Mary, I learned a long time ago to say, 'Whatever, Lord.' And this is just another 'Whatever.'"

After they took you to surgery, we returned to your room, and that was the hardest part, because then you weren't there with us to keep us laughing.

A Little Less Brain, a Lot More Hope
The surgery went well. The doctors performed a right frontal lobectomy, examining the tumor and taking samples for the biopsy and testing. When it was all over, I woke up with a wiry row of staples and sutures forming a headband over my scalp from one ear to the other.

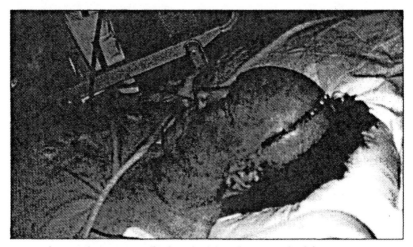

The craniotomy required an incision that stretched from ear to ear. Afterward I was left with a line of staples that resembled a barbed-wire headband. It looked terrible but was nearly painless.

Amazingly, there was never any pain. Jokingly, I explained to my friends that it was because I have a numb skull. But the really amazing thing was that the craniotomy was done under local anesthesia! The doctors didn't want me to be heavily sedated because they weren't sure how my brain would respond. So I was awake, sort of, so that initially I could hear what the surgical team was saying—and it scared me! Two of the doctors were discussing the advantages of wearing a belt versus a belt with suspenders! I kept wanting to say, "Hey! I'm having brain surgery here! Could you please forget about what's holding up your pants for a while? Let's focus on the brain surgery, gentlemen: FOCUS!"

Apparently, they were able to do brain surgery and discuss apparel issues at the same time, because the surgery went well. Afterward, however, the doctors told me the tumor was too deeply embedded in my brain to be surgically removed. But there was some good news, too. They had identified the tumor as lymphoma, a kind of cancer they said they knew how to treat. In fact, one of them bravely predicted that I had an 85 percent chance of making a complete recovery. During the next few days following the surgery, they would work in the laboratory, treating samples of the tumor with various combinations of chemo drugs until they found the right "cocktail," as they called it, that would melt the tumor.

Interpreting the News
As I've said many times, my husband, Bill, is a melancholy personality, one of those eternal pessimists who see the dark cloud within every silver lining. On the evening of my surgery, when the neurosurgeon came out of the operating room and told my family and friends, "This is good news. The cancer is a kind that is highly treatable and responsive to chemotherapy," Bill threw his hands up in despair. "That's it," he said. "She won't be traveling with Women of Faith anymore. This is the end of all the traveling and speaking. Just forget that."

Mary Graham calmly patted Bill's hand and said, "Bill, that's not what I heard the doctor say. He said Barb's cancer is responsive to chemotherapy and treatable. I don't think you should rule out anything yet."

Sheila reinforced Mary's remarks. "Bill, this is Barb we're talking about! Just think what God has brought her through. No tumor will determine when her time on this earth is over; only Jesus will. I think of the millions of lives she has touched, and I don't believe God is finished with her yet."

Then they prayed, thanking God for the life I'd been given so far, for wonderful doctors, and for the perfect love of God that casts out fear. They lifted me up into the strong arms I've rested in for so many years.

As they prayed, a short way down the hall, I was being wheeled into the intensive care ward. The next chapter of my life had begun.

Was I Strange?

Several times during my recovery from the surgery, nurses would come into my room and ask me, "Mrs. Johnson? How are you feeling? Do you know where you are?"

Their questions always surprised me. How dumb did they think I was? It was stenciled right there in big black letters on the front of my hospital gown: St. Jude's Medical Center. If I did forget where I was, all I had to do was look at my chest, and there was the answer!

Later I remembered that handy reminder when a friend sent me this funny note:

You were a particular blessing to me when I was diagnosed with breast cancer two years ago. I knew God would bring me out the other side better than when I started, and Barb, you play a big part in helping me feel that way. I was able to joke and laugh when other people thought I was going crazy. But when God is in control He can help you see some of the comical things that happen.

After my surgeries—the mastectomy, reconstruction, and then laparoscopic removal of adhesions—I now have a wonderful happy face on my abdomen. When there are

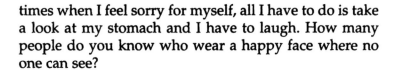

times when I feel sorry for myself, all I have to do is take a look at my stomach and I have to laugh. How many people do you know who wear a happy face where no one can see?

Despite my assurances that I had felt fine before the tumor was discovered and that I remembered who I was and where I was after the surgery, the doctors continued the quizzing as the days went by. They said that tumors like mine often interfered with thought processes or creative ability. Again and again they asked me if my friends and family had noticed that I had mentally slipped in the last few weeks. "No one's said anything," I told them. "But maybe they've just been too polite to notice."

I asked my son David if he had noticed any change in my conversation. He said, "Well, you do repeat things a lot, but then you *always* did that!" (I guess all mothers feel they have to say things at least *twice* to be sure the kids understand what has to be done.)

Next I called my friends and told them the doctors wanted to know if I had been acting strange recently. I urged them to be honest and tell me the truth, no matter how hard it would be for me to hear.

"How would we know, Barb?" one friend replied. "You've *always* been a little strange."

One of my traveling companions mused over the question awhile and then said, "Well, when we were in Omaha, you collected all the miniature bottles of ketchup off all the room-service trays left out in the hotel hallway. But you've done that for years."

"And *you* took the baby-sized jars of jelly," I pointedly reminded her.

"You got stopped by a police cruiser when you were out walking around Tulsa in the middle of the night," another helper continued.

"But when he found out I was on my way to the all-night Wal-Mart, he gave me a lift," I replied. "And I wasn't just going shopping in the middle of the night. I was trying to find a typewriter so I could write about something that had happened that day. It was too long to write out in longhand, and I wanted to remember it for my next book."

"There was that time you tore off a piece of an evergreen bush at the post office and told the next guy in line it was beginning to taste a lot like Christmas," another pal remembered. "But that was years ago."

"You got lost in that huge mall in Birmingham and couldn't remember which door you came in," another helper reminded me.

"But you were with me! And you couldn't remember which door we came in either. At least *I* remembered we came in near a mannequin wearing a purple dress."

"Right, and a lot of good that did us when we turned ourselves into the information desk, asking for help," she grumbled defensively.

Obviously, my friends weren't going to be a lot of help in this area. When I told the doctors no one seemed to have noticed anything different, they didn't seem to know whether to be relieved or skeptical.

"It's just amazing that you have a tumor this size and yet your memory and your behavior don't seem to have been affected," one of them told me.

"Well, I'm just glad you're not telling me to keep on asking my friends if I've been acting strange," I admitted. "After listening to them, I'm starting to think I've been crazy a long, long time!"

Absent-mindedly, I lifted my pen up to scratch my ear.

"Don't do that!" the surgeon suddenly commanded. "You might push it all the way through!"

I gasped and dropped my pen.

"Just kidding," he said with a laugh, patting my hand.

The Healing Gift of Laughter
How thankful I've been this year to have wonderful doctors with a great sense of humor as well as plenty of friends and

family members who love to laugh, too. While I was in the hospital and in the months since I've been home, enduring chemotherapy and endless scans and physical therapy, I've been overwhelmed by an avalanche of mail from well-wishers and Women of Faith attendees. All the cards and letters are appreciated—even the ones accompanied by handfuls of glitter and bits of confetti that sprinkled all over the carpet when I opened them. (I could appreciate them since Bill did all the housework and vacuuming while I recuperated.) But I was especially grateful for the funny cards and the letters that included stories about the writers' own calamities and misadventures as well as inspiring insights. Many of them had nothing to do with cancer or get-well wishes. They were just laughable stories the writers offered as a get-well gift to me. And of course I want to share those laughs with *you*.

For example, Pat Swarthout from Pennsylvania wrote to tell me about the time she fell into her aunt's sunken grave during a wintertime visit when the cemetery was covered with snow. "I went in the grave up to my knee and broke my ankle. My brother pulled me out. I felt like a nut in the emergency room when they asked how the accident happened. I had to say, 'Well, I fell in my aunt's grave.'"

Now, there are two ways to look at such an experience. You can mope around and feel embarrassed at having fallen into a grave. Or you can laugh. Pat was sharing this story with me, she wrote, "because when this happened I was reading in one of your books a quote that said, 'Any day above ground is a good one.' I thought, *How fitting*. And now at Easter time I can really sing, 'Up from the grave I arose.' . . . When I sing that hymn, I know how it feels to be pulled up from the grave. I also know I *will* rise up from the grave again someday."

Pat is also a cancer survivor, and in addition to her broken ankle she has endured several other painful conditions. But none of these ailments keeps her from sharing joy wherever she goes (she loves to serve *square*-shaped deviled eggs to her friends), so she's always on the lookout for funny things.

During her recovery from cancer, she had radiation treatments for thirty-five days in a row. That might have been enough to dampen the spirits of someone who wasn't so attuned to humorous situations—but not Pat. She carries a camera with her everywhere she goes, so one day when she was driving to another radiation treatment and spotted an unusual sight amid some road construction, she was ready to record it. A portable toilet had been placed on the roadside, right next to a big sign that said, "Emergency Stopping Only." She laughed out loud—then whipped out her camera, snapped the photograph, and sent it to me. "I thought you'd get a kick out of this," she wrote.

As she drove to and from radiation treatments, Pat Swarthout was always looking for joy gems to photograph. When she noticed where the road-construction crew had placed their portable toilet, she grabbed her camera—and recorded her laugh for the day.

Pat describes herself as someone who "can have a sense of humor and yet experience rough times," including progressive arthritis, fibromyalgia, diverticulitis, and breast cancer. Yet she focuses on the good things that happen to her and seeks out humorous moments in the world around her. And best of all, she shares the joy she finds. My favorite part of her letter came in her motto at the end:

> I hurt if I do.
> I hurt if I don't do.
> So I *do* do.

Lisa Wharry also shared a funny story, saying, "If it brings even a glimmer of light or laughter, it's the least I can do for you, seeing as how you and your books were the vehicle God used to save my sanity during one of the most difficult times I've ever had to face."

Like so many of my own experiences, Lisa's began with trauma. Her family's beloved dog, Mucky, a playful white mutt with a big, black head, was mostly a house dog, but she had an uncanny way of sneaking outside whenever the door was open—including those times in the wee morning hours when the cats demanded to go outside.

Lisa was driving her daughter to school one morning when they turned onto the main thoroughfare a couple of blocks from their house and found their precious Mucky lying dead on the pavement. "One look at that giant black head, twisted and mangled though it was, and there was no denying this was the puppy we had rescued from the streets five years ago," Lisa wrote.

She picked up the poor dog's lifeless body and placed it in the backseat of her car, noticing how much heavier it seemed than when the dog would playfully jump onto her lap and snuggle with her.

Back home, she called her mother and sister to come and hear the sad news and to help her dig a grave for Mucky in the backyard.

The women were in shock, hearing this news so early in the

morning. But Lisa's sister was especially stunned. "I just put her in the bathroom a few minutes ago," she exclaimed. Lisa knew a few minutes could mean anything to her sister, depending on how much sleep she'd had, and Lisa didn't have the heart to argue. "It was just one of those times when you want to smack someone. I guess she sensed that, because she finally gave up and went into the house."

Just as Lisa and her mother were lifting Mucky's body from the backseat of the car, they heard the sister's muffled cry. They left the dog and ran into the house.

"There stood Mucky with the biggest, dopiest grin plastered all over her big black face, her entire body wagging behind her."

Then it suddenly dawned on Lisa that she had someone else's dead dog in the backseat of her car.

"We tried, to no avail, to find the owner. Ultimately we had a private funeral, complete with a 5' x 2' x 2' grave and prayer before interment. But not before we noticed what a handsome young *male* dog this had been."

Lisa's bittersweet story brought a moment of humor, as well as a little lesson in grace. "This poor dog that looked like Mucky died a death that could have been Mucky's, just as Jesus—God in our clothes—died a death that, but for the grace of God, should have been ours," she wrote.

And then she signed off with this bit of encouragement:

> *Keep your chin up.*
> *And when it gets too heavy, God will*
> *send His angels to hold it up for you!*

A friend in North Dakota sent this advice: "Barbara, when I was sick with cancer someone gave me *Stick a Geranium in Your Hat and Be Happy!* Maybe you should read it and get the same enjoyment out of it you gave me in a tough time."

Another woman, also a cancer survivor, encouraged me, "You will get through this, so just . . .

Hang on to your bootstraps and keep on walking.

**A friend sent me a card that said, "Barb,
when I count my blessings, you're right up there!"**

Another friend sent a little box of raisins with a note that said:

> Barb, I'm raisin you up in prayer!

And Olga Fairfax, who, by the way, holds a Ph.D., sent me a funny story about herself after she'd read a ridiculous joke in one of my books about a man who was totally absorbed in watching a televised football game while his wife was ironing nearby. When she left the room and the phone rang, he grabbed the iron instead of the phone and scorched the side of his head with it! When the doctor asked how *both* sides of his head got burned, he replied, "I had no sooner hung up than the fool called back!"

Well, Olga read that story, and I guess her ears really burned! She wrote to tell me:

> I am the original source for the "ironing my face" story in your book. About thirty years ago whenever I talked to

my mother on the phone, I did my ironing. One day, while I was ironing a linen tablecloth (which used the hottest setting—my iron went from one to twelve, and I had it set on thirteen!), I put the phone down momentarily, turned around, and then picked up the IRON and laid it on my cheek! It was scalding! I grabbed ice but the next day my cheek had a perfect outline of the iron! Every child and teacher at the school where I taught art remarked about the red mark. That afternoon, the principal called me into his office. With an absolutely straight face, he asked me, "You did WHAT?" He said that that is all he had heard about all day—Mrs. Fairfax ironing her face.

Passing on the Blessings
Throughout my illness, friends and readers have sent me a multitude of gifts—flowers, candy, lotion, bubble bath—you wouldn't believe the variety of things that have poured into my house. But the gifts I've appreciated most are the laughter-filled stories and jokes that have brightened my day with chuckles. And best of all, I get to pass them on to *you*, so the gift becomes my favorite thing: a boomerang blessing!

When my cancer was diagnosed, we were in the process of putting together a new book that would focus on our work in Spatula Ministries, an outreach that helps hurting parents who have landed on the ceiling due to some catastrophe involving their children. We like to say Spatula peels these parents off the ceiling with a spatula of love and sets them on the road to recovery.

After my craniotomy, so many friends remembered the story about the reader mixing up the title of my first *Geranium* book and calling it *Stick a Geranium in Your Cranium*, it seemed only natural that the next book would have to have a *cranium* link and include my reluctant role as a "dancer with cancer." Finally, we settled on the idea of *planting* a geranium in your cranium with the subtitle *Sowing Seeds of Joy in the Manure of Life*. I just love the idea of joyful things that *grow* out of the crises that fertilize our lives!

Now, you may be familiar with past episodes of how I've tormented my dear friends at W Publishing Group (formerly Word Publishing) with my stubborn insistence about putting words in the titles of my books that make publishers' hair turn gray and fall out (which, after completing chemotherapy, I no longer think is funny). This time, the word *manure* gave them a few breathless moments. But after publishing a dozen of my wacky titles, this time those good folks gave in without too much fuss. And as soon as the title was announced, my friends started sending me comments and clippings about manure.

For example one of them sent me a story about a Florida legislator who sent a gift-wrapped bag of manure to a lobbyist to express her feelings about the lobbyist's position. I thought, *That's just how I feel about this cancer. I'm sure something good will come out of it, and maybe someday I'll be able to see the gift in it—but right now . . . it stinks!*

Someone else sent me a little reminder that

We are most open to Jesus in the tough times of life.
The fertilizer of good soil never smells good.

And that reminded me of what my daughter-in-love, Shannon, has said for years, that it's down in life's valleys that we grow, "because that's where the fertilizer is."

Finally, someone else sent me a little quip from *Prairie Home Companion* that doesn't make a lot of sense to me—but it does make me laugh, so who cares if it makes sense!

Remember, when the chips are down
the buffalo is empty.

Not Merely Surviving, but Surviving Joyfully
As much as I love sharing all the bits of love and silliness that encouraged me during this ordeal, I don't want you to think I'm saying that having cancer is a breeze—just smile and be happy and everything will be fine. In fact, it's awful. So don't think there was any courage on my part; I was just facing what was put before me.

Most people step up to the plate and endure the
ties because they have no other choice; they just have to bite u ιc
bullet and get through it. Hearing someone tell you that you
have cancer isn't good news. But it isn't the end of your life,
either, unless you *choose* to stop living it! In many cases, cancer
is now considered a chronic disease rather than a fatal one.

Taking charge of your emotions, gathering medical information, and approaching life with a positive, faith-filled attitude is the key to dealing creatively with cancer. Find the
goodness and the humor in everything around you. Don't let
despair take over. Let the cancer diagnosis—or whatever the
shocking news that has been delivered to you—be the catalyst
that leads you to reevaluate yourself and your relationship
with others. Let it impel you to draw more than ever on your
inner strengths and your faith. Instead of asking, "Why me?"
ask, "What can I learn from this experience?"

When you have cancer, you feel apprehensive during the
months of chemotherapy or other treatments. You may lose
your hair, eyelashes, and eyebrows, and you're nauseous and
depressed for days on end. And yet you know inside your heart
that you will come through to the other side—either health or
heaven—and that gives you the strength to endure. Then when
you do, everyone wants to pin a star on your chest as though
you've accomplished some amazing feat that you volunteered
for. The truth is, of course, it was not your choice. No one would
ever choose cancer. But with God's help we merely endure; no
medal is in order. Surviving is merely a job to be done.

Of course, any job's always easier when it's done joyfully—and gratefully. Sometimes—when we're diagnosed
with a serious illness, for example—we don't feel like being
grateful. Or we may feel ashamed that we are so needy,
ashamed to acknowledge the help we have already received
and the help we will need in the future. Oh, but if we can get
past that shameful obstacle and for *all* things give thanks,
what a difference it makes in our lives.

God doesn't really need our gratitude, but *we* need to be
grateful! A thankful heart deepens our faith and enhances the

quality of our lives. That's why we need to turn to God on sunny days as well as those times when storms and crises wreck our lives. Counting our blessings is a sure way to enrich our daily journey. Tally up your simple blessings and simple treasures every chance you get. Write them down and marvel at how long the list grows. Develop the habit of thankfulness, and it will lead to a life of optimistic thinking.

When I was in chemotherapy, I counted the pills I was required to take in a twenty-four-hour period. It was up to eighty! About half of them had nice, smooth coating on them—like M&Ms—and I thanked God sincerely for those slick ones that were easier to swallow. It was such a little thing, but if you look for tiny blessings, you'll find them everywhere. Even in an assortment of pills to be swallowed. When your feelings are raw and your heart is heavy, consciously and willfully choose to give thanks. You'll find that you grow in love as you grow in gratefulness.

Billy Graham has said that God has given us two hands—one to receive with and the other to give with. When both hands are busy, we have balance and serenity. All of us are carrying burdens of one kind or another. Sometimes it seems we're so consumed with our own problems, so needy and helpless, we can't think of any way we can give anyone anything. When you reach that point, remember the one thing you can *always* give. You can give thanks!

Moments of Mirth in the Manure Pile

Cancer is the manure pit of life. But I know God is there in the pit with me, and He can use that ugly mess to fertilize my life with love and hope. And laughter!

Dr. William Bucholz told the story of overhearing two physicians discussing a paper they were to deliver at a national meeting of cancer specialists. One was complaining bitterly, "I don't understand it, Bob. We use the same drugs, the same dosage, and the same schedule of treatment. Yet I get a 22 percent recovery rate, and you get a 74 percent recovery rate. How do you explain that?"

The other responded, "We both use Etoposide, Platinol, Oncovin, and Hydroxyurea. You put those letters together and tell people that you are giving them EPOH. I put them together and explain to them that they are receiving HOPE. I emphasize that they have a chance."[3]

Life is very simple: It merely consists in learning how to accept the impossible, how to do without the indispensable, how to endure the insupportable.

—KATHLEEN NORRIS

NON SEQUITUR   By Wiley

One of my friends told me her sister had also had surgery when a brain tumor was removed. At one point after the surgery, her doctor failed to tell her about an important test result, and the sister fumed, "I'd just like to give that doctor a piece of my mind."

Then she paused a moment and considered where she was and why she was there. "Oh," she said. "I guess I already have!"

Do not be surprised at the painful trial you are suffering, as though something strange were happening to you. But rejoice that you participate in the sufferings of Christ, so that you may be overjoyed when his glory is revealed. (1 Peter 4:12–13)

This would be funny
if it weren't happening to *me*

If all is not lost . . . where IS it?

Wearing a barbed-wire headband is not my idea of fun—or fashion. So as soon as I was able, I started doing something about it: whining. At one point, my doctor, probably tired of hearing me complain yet again about my prickly scalp, looked me right in the eye and said earnestly, "Mrs. Johnson, we can't take out the sutures and staples too soon. Your face might fall off!"

Well! That shut me up.

Then he smiled, of course. Still, my hand went instinctively to my face. I gave it a gentle touch, making sure it was securely connected to my head.

My friend Steve Arterburn put a more positive spin on my wired scalp. "I've got a great idea, Barb," he told me, trying to count the number of staples holding my face onto my head. "You could be the spokesperson for an office-supply store!"

My hospital stay lasted longer than I had expected, but finally the day came when I was wheeled out of the hospital and into the car. Then Bill and our two sons, David and Barney, and Barney's wife, Shannon, welcomed me back home. Oh,

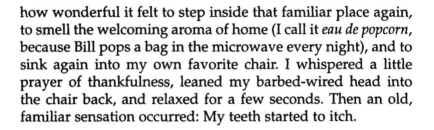

how wonderful it felt to step inside that familiar place again, to smell the welcoming aroma of home (I call it *eau de popcorn*, because Bill pops a bag in the microwave every night), and to sink again into my own favorite chair. I whispered a little prayer of thankfulness, leaned my barbed-wired head into the chair back, and relaxed for a few seconds. Then an old, familiar sensation occurred: My teeth started to itch.

From Laundry Room to Launch Pad

"Bill's got a surprise for you," Shannon said, her beautiful face beaming with anticipation.

"A surprise?" I said, imagining all sorts of possibilities from jewelry to Joy Room additions.

Shannon handed me a videocassette. *Oh,* I thought, suddenly feeling tears of gratitude welling up in my eyes, *my family has put together some sort of video get-well card, one of those sentimental collections of I-love-you's with photos and tributes and . . .*

Then I read the cover of the cassette. It said something like "Operating Your New Computerized Maytag Neptune Washer and Dryer." I looked at Shannon, wondering why they hadn't used a *new* cassette for the video tribute instead of taping over some advertising film.

"Barb, Bill bought you a new washer and dryer," she said sweetly, her gorgeous brown eyes sparkling, "the top-of-the-line models. You won't believe all the things they can do. We all knew what a chore it was for you to use that old washer and dryer. Why, that dryer hardly worked at all, and the washer was on its last legs. It didn't spin at all. It just grunted and groaned."

"A new washer and dryer?" I asked.

"Yes! Come see it!" Shannon bubbled, helping me out of the chair. Bill and Barney were waiting in the laundry room beside two glistening white machines topped with elaborate, computerized control panels. I felt like I'd stepped into the space shuttle cockpit.

"Ohhhh," I said, desperately wanting to run my hand nervously over my head—but encountering the barbed-wire headband instead. "Th-that's nice. How do they work?"

"That's what the video's for," Bill said, beaming like a proud papa. "You have to watch the video, and it tells you how to run 'em."

"I have to watch a video to learn how to do the laundry?" During nearly two weeks of my hospital stay, despite brain surgery and having a barbed-wire fence implanted in my scalp, I hadn't felt one moment of pain. Now a headache threatened to rumble up from somewhere near my spleen. "B-but, where are my *old* washer and dryer?"

"Oh, they hauled 'em off when they brought the new ones," Bill said with a dismissive wave of his hand.

"You hauled them off?" I could hear my voice shifting into whining mode again. "But, Bill, I *liked* my old washer and dryer. I sure don't feel up to watching a video to learn how to wash my clothes."

"Well, you don't have to watch it *now*," he said a little huffily. "I'll do the laundry until you get back on your feet again. You're not gonna be doing *any* housework for a while."

Amazingly, my headache suddenly vanished.

"I'd trade it in if it weren't for all the socks still unaccounted for."

Paradise Lost

Things had changed while I'd been away. Papers I'd left scattered around my desk, on my nightstand, and beside my chair were now neatly stacked on a dresser. Pieces of mail I'd left out to answer were put away, somewhere out of sight. Book proposals, publishers' faxes, and Women of Faith correspondence I'd been working on had all been relocated to neater, tidier stacks and baskets. My house looked perfect— clean as a whistle and so orderly and organized Martha Stewart would be proud.

I was furious.

Every time I looked for something and couldn't find it, my frustration built until I would have pulled my hair out, if I'd had any. "I can't find *anything!*" I fussed while my family ran for cover.

"It's all here, Barb," Bill insisted. "I made sure nothing important got thrown out."

"Then where *is* it?" I fumed again and again, on the trail of some crucially important bit of paper.

"It'll turn up," Bill reassured me before making a quick exit.

Fighting the Limits

Finally the wire sutures and staples were removed, and my mood improved a little. But there were still major moments of irritation. In between searching for lost items, I answered the phone, which rang constantly. Bill said we should just let the answering machine kick in, but when we did, the caller would leave a message, and I'd overhear the familiar voice and want to talk to that person. Eventually, Bill put the word out that we appreciated the love and prayers but we just couldn't answer the phone right now. And others spread the word that friends shouldn't call.

"But I *need* contact with my friends," I argued with Bill and with my family, who seemed to be urging me to somehow put myself into a bubble—or a coma. So the phone calls resumed. And yet, I grew so tired of repeating the same things—describing my hospital stay and the frightening brain surgery, my slowly returning strength, my latest doctor's follow-up exam, all laced with pointed remarks about the new computerized washer and dryer. There were times during the phone conversations when I wanted to say, "One moment, please" and connect the caller to a prerecorded message giving my latest health and mood update.

And some of the calls, despite the callers' good intentions, weren't all that cheerful. One couple called me to send their love and added that they had a friend who had endured the same condition a year or so earlier.

"Oh," I said, "how's she doing now?"

There was a silent pause. "Well," the husband answered, "she can't talk, walk, or see . . ." Then he hurried to add, "But she's still hanging in there."

Well, I thought, hanging up the receiver after saying goodbye, *THAT was cheerful!*

"Please stay on the line. We're trying to set a Guinness world record."

Already feeling weakened and disoriented by the surgery, I knew an even darker cloud hung over my future. In a couple of weeks, as soon as I recovered from the surgery and my blood pressure could be stabilized, I would be facing several weeks of chemotherapy. Remembering all the stories I'd heard about chemo over the years, I imagined myself feeling bad and bald, suffering a months-long bout of nausea and depression.

Slowly I sensed that the Geranium Lady, whose lifework in the last two decades had been helping others find joy amid the cow patties of life's pasture, was sinking into the manure pit herself.

Words of Encouragement
The mail generated feelings of encouragement—and failure. For years Bill has collected our mail each day in a basket supplied by the post office. His job has always been to bring it home, open it, and send receipts for any donations that come in to Spatula Ministries. My job has been to answer the letters and respond to the pleas for help. Whenever I could, I tried to make a phone call or send a note and respond to as many letters as possible.

But as news of my brain surgery leaked out, the mail started pouring in. In one day alone, Bill brought home several hundred cards and letters. But I wasn't feeling up to opening them that day or the next, so very quickly, the mail began piling up. Sometimes I looked at the baskets of mail stacked on top of each other, awaiting my attention, and felt a glow of strengthening warmth, knowing the envelopes held messages of hope. Other times, I watched the mail stacks grow with a deepening sense of despair, thinking, *I'll never get through all those letters.*

The worst part was knowing that a few of the letters weren't from well-wishers. They were from hurting parents who hadn't heard of my brain tumor and were asking for help themselves, pouring out their own pain. Those were the letters, left unread, that bothered me the most. Yet for the first time since our ministry began, I felt unable to read the mail, let alone respond. Barbara Johnson, the woman who had cherished for years God's incredible gift of boundless energy, couldn't muster the emotional fortitude to open a single envelope. While holding on to hope, I nonetheless lapsed into lethargy.

It's Not As Bad As You Think

Interestingly, about this time, a couple of friends faxed me the same wire service story clipped from different newspapers. It described cancer patients who had been through chemotherapy and found it wasn't nearly as bad as they had expected. One of the women quoted said, "It was no walk in the park, but I was still able to work, be a mom, be a wife. What I had in my mind and what I lived through were entirely different. . . . I never threw up. The medicine was amazing. I was sicker with the flu. It's not as bad as you think."[1]

The article was encouraging, but I wasn't totally convinced. And I worried that chemo would take away what little strength I had managed to hang on to after the surgery.

My doctor listened patiently to the recitation of my woes and patted my shoulder, "It's okay, Barb. You'll have time for all the mail and phone calls later. Right now your priority is to get well. So I'm giving you a new prescription. It's not for a medication. It's for rest. In the next few weeks we have to build up your body and get it as strong as we can before we

ZIGGY   **By Tom Wilson**

start the chemo. So here's what I want you to do: Get plenty of rest and only do the things you really enjoy doing. Just do what *you* want to do—your favorite things—that's *all* you're allowed to do."

A Failure at Favorites

Okay, let's see. What are my favorite things to do? I asked myself as I drove home from the doctor's office. Well, hands down, my favorite thing is putting together our Spatula Ministries newsletter. But we already had the next month's issue done, and the following month's issue was just about finished, too, so that was out. My next favorite thing is traveling with my Women of Faith friends and meeting all the enthusiastic women around the country who flock to the conferences. But obviously, I wasn't going to be traveling for a while. *Hmmmm,* I mused as I drove home, feeling my emotions sliding back down into the gutter. *This relaxing and doing favorite things isn't going to be easy.*

By the time I got home, I had thought of something wild and wonderful—something I *really* wanted to do. I marched resolutely into the kitchen, took an industrial-sized box of cereal out of the cupboard, and dumped it in the trash. Bill, my penny-pinching partner, rounded the corner just as the last flake was fluttering into the trash can.

"What are you doing?" he asked, eyes wide, eyebrows lifted.

"The doctor told me to do it," I answered.

"He told you to pour out a perfectly good box of cereal?"

"He told me to do whatever I wanted to do for the next few weeks while I get ready for the chemo. We bought this fifty-five-gallon drum of cereal at the warehouse club, and I've never liked it. I'll be dead before I eat it all, Bill. I don't like it, and I don't want to eat it, and the doctor told me to do anything I wanted, and *this* is what I decided I wanted to do. So I did it," I stated emphatically, folding my arms for emphasis and catching a glimpse of my determined image reflected in the door of the microwave. My partially bald head was gleaming under the kitchen light. (It's so hard to be dignified when your scalp is glowing like a streetlight.)

"Oh, brother!" Bill muttered and headed out the door.

Let the Treatments Begin!

Now that my strength was returning, it became more difficult to rest. There were so many things I wanted to do—visit my friends, answer the mail, run the usual errands. But each time I attempted these things, I felt my energy evaporating, and soon I was exhausted, almost too weak to stand. Eventually, I gave in to the doctor's orders, closing the shades, unplugging the phone, and settling back into bed. It was a very pleasant feeling.

BUCKLES By David Gilbert

Reprinted with special permission of King Features Syndicate

Finally, the doctors declared I was strong enough to start the chemotherapy. What mixed emotions surged through me as I absorbed the news! Surely it's akin to the feelings the Thanksgiving turkey would have if it knew why it was being fattened up in early November. In essence I was being told that I was now healthy enough to have my body loaded up with poisons. Oh, goody!

The preparations began seventy-two hours before the first chemotherapy treatment. As the doctor described the regimen I was to follow, I couldn't believe my ears. Every three hours, all night long, I had to drink thirteen ounces of water and take six pills.

"Every three hours! Oh, I can't do that," I protested. "And I hate taking pills."

"You can do it," Bill interrupted. "I'll remind you. You'll do it!"

"Oh, brother!" I sighed, heading out the bedroom door.

And so we began. Bill sorted twenty-four hours' worth of pills into a muffin tin. Then he set the alarm clock and showed up every three hours at my bedside with the muffin tin and a carefully measured glass of cold water. Later he bought a case of bottled water and kept it and the muffin tin on his side of the bed during the night. Every three hours, he nudged me awake, loosened the cap of the bottled water, and sat beside me, watching to make sure I swallowed all the pills and every drop of those thirteen ounces of water.

"You don't have to watch me," I told him petulantly.

"Oh, yes I do," he answered stoutly. "You've gotta drink thirteen ounces of water and take all of these pills, and I'm gonna make sure you do it."

"Bill, I've decided," I told him late on the second night, after thirty-six hours of nonstop water drinking and pill popping every three hours, "I don't want to do this. I've decided I just want to sleep and forget the pills. Forget the chemo. I just want to sleep."

"Oh, no you don't," he bristled. "You take these pills, and you drink this water, and in three hours we'll do it again."

Bill, a former lieutenant commander in the navy, can have

a very authoritative presence when he's not being a lovable teddy bear of a guy. I almost saluted and shouted, "Aye, aye, sir!" before morosely taking the muffin tin from him, digging out the latest batch of pills, tossing them into my mouth, and gulping down the water. I could hear and feel the liquid sloshing in my stomach as I padded to the bathroom, my permanent headquarters during this regimen.

What Am I Doing Here?
After an eternity of swallowing pills and chugging water, the day of my first chemo treatment dawned. During my prayers that morning, I flipped through the Bible, looking for an empowering verse to take with me. I chose as my carry-along verse the ancient, uplifting words of Joshua:

> Be strong and courageous. Do not be terrified; do not be discouraged, for the LORD your God will be with you wherever you go.[2]

As if to emphasize that promise, my eyes happened to pass over a couple of letters lying on my desk. One was a note faxed to me from my friend Debbie Wickwire. She wrote,

> I went to sleep last night and woke up this morning praying for you. I'm seeing Jesus sitting beside your chemo chair . . .

Long ago when my life was mired in the manure pit, I started collecting funny jokes and pictures to lift my spirits. The collection started out in a shoebox and later got its own addition built on to our home! It's my Joy Room, and I spend lots of time there, soaking up all the love and fun I've stockpiled over the years.

When my cancer was diagnosed, the Joy Room collection grew even larger as friends sent the funny cartoons and spirit-lifters they knew I craved. On that morning before my first chemo treatment, I took a moment to look through the latest stack of silly quips and heart-touching sentiments. Standing guard over the latest arrivals was a funny little ceramic figure—a merry-looking, hospital-gown-clad Geranium Lady, her head shaved and her scalp crisscrossed with Xs representing the wire stitches and staples that had held my face on, according to my doctor. A friend had made it for me after seeing the photographs of my postsurgical hairdo in the hospital.

One friend, knowing I dreaded the chemo treatments (despite the news reports that their side effects were no longer so harsh), reminded me of Jesus' words related to the Great Commission:

> These signs will accompany those who believe: . . . when they drink deadly poison, it will not hurt them at all.[3]

Another writer reminded me that my job now was simply to cuddle into God's loving protection and grace:

> Your part is to just rest in the loving arms of God. Like Corrie ten Boom said, "Don't wrestle, just nestle."

What a comforting image! And right under that note was another one from a friend who said, "Isn't God awesome, Barb? He has a permanent indent of you under His wing!" That thought reminded me of the time Bill and I made reservations at a Mennonite tourist home. They signed their return letter to us, "Under the same feathers." Now, thinking of nestling in the Father's arms, pressing an indent of myself under His wing, I thought, *How true. He gathers us under His wings as a hen gathers her chicks for protection and rest.*

Settling back in my desk chair, I soaked up the words of comfort, and suddenly my heart filled with joy even as I prepared for this dreaded ordeal. Here's a sampling of the humorous notes I savored that day:

> Keep your *chins* up, Barb! (I speak from experience—told my grandson the other day I'm part iguana.)

Barb, since you, too, have had brain surgery, I'd just like to welcome you to the true airheads of America. Twelve years ago I was told I had a brain tumor. . . . It turned out to be a vein leaking blood into the higher-thinking area of my brain. What a relief! As I informed the doctor, I have no high thoughts and would never use that part of my brain anyway!

May perfect health chase you down, Barb, and overtake you—STAT!

B N Kurged (be encouraged)

How many times have I remembered the quip from your book about someone practicing for the Rapture by going into the backyard and jumping on a trampoline. (I can't do that. No trampoline's available and my bladder leaks.) . . . Barbara, you are one of the world's seven wonders! . . . Bless you! Stick a geranium in your panty girdle . . . and giggle.

I still have the little blue crystal stone you gave me. It's a little bruised from the garbage disposal, but it still shines and reminds me of you.

I have a song in my heart and a giggle on my lips for you. . . . Yesterday I was cleaning out the fireplace and I ran a splinter into my finger and out the other side. My family doctor could not remove it, so I made a trip to the hospital. I was so embarrassed, covered in soot from head to toe. Sitting there in the hospital, all embarrassed, I started laughing, thinking what you would do in this situation. Then I began to pray for each one in that room. Thank you, Barb!

> *The lady of humor*
> *Now has a tumor,*
> *But I know she won't be beat.*
> *Her good Shepherd tends her*
> *Wherever He sends her,*
> *And in heaven she already has a seat!*

Barb, I am praying that U will B
"touched in the head" by God!

Then I saw the little pin someone had left at my book table when the Women of Faith conference was in Atlanta. It was metal but resembled a loop of ribbon, crisscrossed, like the pink breast-cancer commemorative pins. But this pin was gray. The woman who gave me the pin was a thirty-nine-year-old cancer survivor. She attached this note to the gift:

Five years ago I was diagnosed with a malig-nant brain tumor. It was the day before my youngest son's second birthday. I never felt despair, even though the surgeon said "no one survives" this kind of brain tumor. He didn't know me and my God! This is a brain tumor awareness pin—gray for "gray matter." Be well, Barb![4]

And then there was my favorite note. It had arrived at my house shortly after a funeral spray of flowers was delivered one day and a condolence card came in the next day's mail. This note said, "Congratulations! The Lord is calling you home. . . . We will miss you, . . . but where you're going is an honor." The poor woman was so embarrassed when she learned later that I actually wasn't expected to die anytime soon, she nearly died herself!

It was so much fun reading all the humorous mail, I was almost late for my chemo appointment.

Laughter in the Chemo Room
The chemotherapy center featured a big room with several comfortable lounge chairs, all sorts of IV racks and other apparatus, and cheerful nurses and staff members who served cookies—and encouragement. But each chair held a solemn-faced person—most of them women—dozing or staring at the walls while the nurses bustled around, tending to the flow lines and checking the IV bags. It instantly struck me that everyone in the room was either bald or wearing a wig or hat of some sort.

As a kindhearted nurse led me to my chair, I had an overwhelming urge to either burst out laughing or dissolve into tears. *"WHAT AM I DOING HERE?"* I wanted to scream. The scene was both terrifying and ridiculous, but I wasn't sure why. Later I realized it's because everyone's wig was slightly (or more than slightly) askew. Bangs had slipped a little bit east or west so that center parts were now running more close to the diagonal. The shorter, curlier styles tended to have slipped backward, leaving their wearers with what looked like seriously receding hairlines.

Right away, remembering my own efforts that morning to get my wig on straight, I understood why. To wear a wig you need to anchor it with bobby pins to your natural hair. And of course, none of us had any! (Well, actually, I had a little. My hair never did fall out, but with the front half shaved, I had no choice but to get the back half cut REALLY short, too.)

After I had settled into a chemo chair and the nurse had hooked me up to the infuser, I commented to the woman in the chair next to mine that we needed an invention to help chemo patients keep their wigs on straight.

"Pantyhose," she said confidently.

Sure she had misunderstood me, I said, "I meant to keep our WIGS from slipping," I said loudly.

"The thing that works best for me is pantyhose," she said again, smiling brightly.

I just smiled and nodded, assuming her brain tumor was a little more advanced than mine. She saw the look and explained: "You cut the legs off then wear the crotch on your head like a cap," she said. "It stays put, and you can pin your wig to the pantyhose."

"Oh!" I said, laughing at the image. Then I had an idea. "We could make a business out of it," I mused. "We could collect the crotches of old pantyhose and sell them as caps to wear under your wig."

(Later a friend even suggested a name for our enterprise: Chemo Crotches!)

There in the chemo room, we erupted into gales of laughter—loud enough to awaken a few of the others whose smiles seemed to have melted beneath their misery. And I'm not sure why, but at that moment I remembered a couple of funny stories from friends.

One was from David Jeremiah, who also underwent surgery due to his bout with lymphoma. He said that two friends had flown all night from California to be with him and his wife before he went into surgery at the Mayo Clinic. Just before he was wheeled off to the OR, they gathered over him to pray, urgently asking God for His powerful protection throughout the ordeal ahead.

Just then a nurse popped into Dr. Jeremiah's room and ordered him to put on a pair of support hose before the surgery commenced to help prevent blood clots and improve circulation. So there they were, helping Dr. Jeremiah wiggle into the support hose, something he had never done before and, I would guess, hopes never to have to do again. It was only a second or two before the somber mood was softened by giggles erupting as the big man wiggled into the skinny hosiery. And then the giggles turned into gales of laughter as the friends pushed and pulled and he twisted and squirmed into the support hose.[5]

And I don't know why, exactly, but the other funny story that came to me that day was one my friend Joyce Heatherley used to tell about a dear woman who lived in a small town. On a beautiful, brisk spring day, she decided to leave her car at home and walk to do her errands. She spent the whole day in the business area of the town, walking from one stop to the next. She paid her light bill and then her telephone bill, went to the post office, had lunch in a little sandwich shop, and stopped by the grocery store before heading home.

It was there, while standing in the checkout line, that a friend came up and said hello. They exchanged pleasantries, then, after giving each other a hug, her friend turned her gently around as she said, "You have something *hanging* on your back." The woman was wearing one of those poodle-cloth coats with the little loops all over it, and something was hanging in the loops on the back of her coat. It was her dirty bra!

I'm not sure what made me think of that particular story that day in the chemo room, except maybe the thought that if we all started wearing pantyhose crotches on our heads, then maybe having our well-worn underwear hanging off our backs would simply be the next easy step toward depravity.

Driving home later, I had to smile, remembering how I had laughed with the lady whose chemo chair was next to mine. Then I recalled my friend Debbie's fax that morning: *I'm seeing Jesus sitting beside your chemo chair . . .*

"Thank You, Lord," I whispered, "for giving me back my bubble of joy in the unlikeliest of places. That's just like You, Jesus, to turn my fear into cheer. Please use me as You used that woman who sat beside me this morning. Help me give some other fearful person the gift of laughter in this journey through my cancer treatment."

Not long after my chemo-room pal and I discussed our pantyhose-crotch business idea, a friend sent me some sticky putty, the stuff you use to hang posters on the wall. "I heard you were having trouble keeping your wig on straight," she joked. "At first I thought of suggesting chewing gum—but thought this might be less messy."

Probably she was just afraid I might forget my wig and go out in public with nothing but a pantyhose crotch on my head!

Wigged Out

It was such fun, thinking of that unexpected chemo-room silliness about wigs, I wanted another helping. Hurrying into the house, I dug through assorted boxes of notes and Joy Room funnies and assembled the collection in a folder I labeled "Wig Wonders." Here are some of my favorite stories, sent to me by my friends:

> When I went through cancer I wore a wig and was still wearing it later when I had ankle surgery. One of our ladies from church was helping me get back together after coming out of the recovery room. She put my wig on me, and when I reached up to see if it was okay, I said, "Irene, you've got it backward."
>
> She said, "Are you sure?" and I answered, "Yes, my bangs don't flip *up*ward!" I tell everyone I'm sure glad she didn't try to put my false teeth in!

> After one round of chemo and surgery I was leaving my surgeon's office where I had received word I would have to have one more round of chemo treatments—at least. My husband was pushing my wheelchair, and I was feeling a wee bit sad. As we waited alone he bent over to hug away the hurt. Upon arighting himself I felt cool air on my bald pate. As I looked back at him to see what on earth he was up to, there hung my hair, attached to his shirt button. Well, I snatched my hair off his chest, sprang from that chair, and charged to the nearest bath-

room. . . . Yes, we'd better have a sense of humor—because God surely does! (Moral: Do not feel sorry for yourself when you have so much to be thankful for.) I'm now cancer free—and I look forward to the time you will be able to say the same.

One of my helpers had forwarded this note from a woman who had stopped by my book table at a Women of Faith conference: "Barb, you know how hot these wigs are. I was driving home from work one day and had stopped at a traffic light. I was so tired and so hot that without thinking I just reached up and pulled off my wig. Then I turned my head and noticed, in the car stopped beside mine, a man carefully shoving his eyeballs back into his head. I guess I scared the poor guy almost out of his mind."

And then someone sent me a GIANT clown wig. It stands nearly a foot high from the top of my head. I laugh out loud every time I pull it on, thinking of all the fun I'm going to have showing up at various gatherings of my friends wearing that wig.

Healing and Humor

Having cancer is not fun. Brain surgery and chemotherapy are a pain. Endless tests and scans and doctor appointments are not causes for laughter. Being cut off from your friends, having your career—your life—interrupted, feeling tired and ill, glimpsing the end of your days on earth . . . these are all reasons why cancer and other life-threatening illnesses can be so devastating. And yet . . . even there, laughter can come bubbling up from deep within the manure pit.

When I was first diagnosed, the doctor gave me a journal to chronicle my trip through this unknown territory, and sometimes, I admit, I've recorded my thoughts as though writing with a pen dipped in tears. But joy is recorded there, too. And I'm enjoying a closer relationship with the One who's making this journey with me, sitting beside me in the next chemo chair, listening to the prayers that come a little more frequently now. One friend described it this way in yet another letter about chemotherapy and hair:

Chemotherapy hair facts . . .

1. Yes, it grows back curly. You won't believe how curly!

2. Then it gets a little wild.

3. Then sometimes it's frizzy.

4. Then suddenly . . . it starts to straighten out.

5. Then you find it's back to normal but thicker, stronger, and changed.

6. God uses your hair as a parable to show you the benefits of the journey.

I would not want to have to make that trip again, Barbara, but I wouldn't have traded the experience for anything, because in it I saw the face of God. He is there.

Her note reminds me of what David Jeremiah wrote in his book *A Bend in the Road*: "Crises never leave us the same as they found us. Those of us who love and trust God through the worst times—those of us who are receptive to what He might be trying to teach us—find that our hearts have changed by the time the stillness replaces the storminess."

Cancer is a storm that transforms the soothing seas of our lives into howling tempests. But Jesus is in the boat with us, and He is all we need. As the comforting lyrics of the wonderful old hymn proclaim:

> *Just when I need Him,*
> *Jesus is near.*
> *Just when I falter,*
> *Just when I fear;*
> *Ready to help me,*
> *Ready to cheer,*
> *Just when I need Him most.*[6]

As David Jeremiah wrote, "The only way *out* is the way *up.* No matter what the problem may be, no matter what trouble may ensnare us, there is only one path to safety. The only hope is to reach beyond ourselves to Someone stronger than we are, and stronger than the shackles that bind us. Only One can fill that requirement."

As another friend said,

When He puts a burden on us,
He puts His arms under us, uplifting us, comforting us.

Of course there's always someone who will quip, as one woman wrote to me:

The Lord gives us no more than He gives us the strength to bear.

Sometimes, though, I wish He didn't have so much confidence in me!

A Message of Reassurance

W Publishing Group maintains thegeraniumlady.com Web site and asked me in the midst of the chemo treatments to send a little update to let everyone know how I was doing. This is the message I sent:

> I'm doing very well. Over the past few weeks I have survived the first round of chemotherapy and am now taking time to heal. I recently read the following prayer that truly explains how I feel:
> "God, give me patience. I thought I was done with the race, but I see there are still several more miles to run. Help me to be thankful for how far I've come. Thank You that You are still continuing to heal me inside and out. Amen."
> I appreciate your thoughts, your prayers, and even the funeral spray of flowers that was mistakenly sent to my house the other day. No, I'm not dead yet!
> I know who I am.
> I know where I am.
> And I know God holds me in the palm of His hand . . .
> He is still on the throne!

Moments of Mirth in the Manure Pile

Let the wind blow your hair . . .
while you still have some.[7]

As I searched for *guidance* I kept seeing "dance" at the end of the word. . . . When I saw "G," I thought of God, followed by "U" and "I."

God, U and I dance.

As I let go and let God, I know that I will get *guidance* in my life . . . when I let God lead.[8]

REAL LIFE ADVENTURES By WISE and ALDRICH

YEAH, I USED TO BE PARANOID ABOUT FINDING HAIR IN THE SINK EVERY MORNING, TOO ... UNTIL I STARTED FINDING NO HAIR IN THE SINK EVERY MORNING.

You don't know what you've got until it's gone.

I refuse to think of them as chin hairs.
I think of them as stray eyebrows.

—JANETTE BARBER

If you can start the day without caffeine or pep pills,
If you can be cheerful, ignoring aches and pains,
If you can resist complaining and boring people
    with your troubles,
If you can understand when loved ones are too
    busy to give you time,
If you can face the world without lies and deceit,
If you can sleep without the aid of drug, then
    . . . you are probably a dog![9]

Remember: You are *not* Martha Stewart. And more than likely she's not coming to your house anytime soon.[10]

Suffering is everywhere. Don't ever think it isn't. So are miracles. Don't ever think they aren't.[11]

A pessimist is one who feels badly when he feels good for fear he'll feel worse when he feels better.[12]

A woman went to her doctor to get the result of a checkup. The doctor said, "I have good news and bad news. Which do you want first?"

She answered, "The good news."

He said, "You have twenty-four hours to live."

"Good grief!" exclaimed the woman. "That's the *good* news? Then what's the *bad* news?"

"The bad news," replied the doctor, "is that I was supposed to tell you yesterday."

It's pretty hard to say what does bring happiness. Poverty and wealth have both failed.[13]

Bibles that are falling apart usually belong to people who are not.[14]

He who sits in the heavens laughs. (Psalm 2:4 NASB)

I'm gonna laugh
about this if it kills me

*Warning: I have an attitude,
and I know how to use it*

after several weeks of chemotherapy, I was back in the oncologist's office for yet another checkup. After enduring half a dozen treatments, it still wasn't clear to me how the chemotherapy was doing its work. So I asked the doctor, "What's happening to the tumor?"

"It's melting," he answered with a reassuring smile.

"Melting? But where is it *going* when it melts?" I hated to sound dumb, but I really wanted to understand what was happening to that pesky blob.

"Well, it melts, and then your body . . . eliminates the residue." He paused a moment and then added, "Barb, just think of it as . . . having a tumor in your bloomers!" As the doctor patted my shoulder and chuckled, I joined in, thankful for a physician who shared my wacky sense of humor.

Fortunately, doctors who practice humor as well as medicine are becoming more plentiful, thanks in part to research that proves the value of laughter in treating illnesses and promoting health. "Doctors and researchers worldwide have found that laughter, a pleasant activity in itself, is good for your health and can be an effective tool in treating a wide range of illnesses," one report stated.[1] The idea got a big boost a few years ago when the movie *Patch Adams* told the true story of a zany young doctor who treated his patients with love and laughter, even going so far as to open his own humor-filled clinic, the Gesundheit Hospital, in West Virginia.

Now another group is studying how to harness classic movie comedies as healing tools. The study is being led by a TV-comedy executive and two UCLA doctors with a "dream team" of advisers—the adult children of Charlie Chaplin, Harpo Marx, W. C. Fields, and Lou Costello. Bill Marx, Harpo's son, shared one of the lessons he had learned from his famous father: "When you have a sense of humor, you automatically have an option in your view of life. Dad always told me, 'A sense of humor is the only weapon you're born with.'"[2]

Other UCLA researchers are looking at ways to utilize humorous TV and movie clips to reduce pain. One report said the study was investigating this hypothesis: What if something that makes you feel good can stop you from feeling bad?[3]

While the scientists are doing these serious studies about humor, you and I can go on our merry way, laughing at every opportunity. For example, on the very day the doctor and I laughed about the whereabouts of my disappearing tumor, I laughed again as I drove home when my eyes fell on a big sign in a florist's window. Advertising a sale on its beautiful fresh flowers, the shop's sign proclaimed:

We've dropped our bloomers for you!

In these turbulent times, we all need humor in large doses just to get through each day, no matter what challenges we face. Laughter gives us the boost we need to carry on, whether we're battling cancer or corralling kids or running a country. As former senator Bob Dole said in a recent interview, "Second only to backbone, every president requires a funny bone." Laughter, said Dole, gives us all "an emotional safety valve," "a sense of proportion," and "an antidote to tears."[4]

On the Lookout for Laughter
A sense of humor is a key component of a life filled with joy and optimism. C. S. Lewis wrote about being *Surprised by Joy,* but I've found that waiting around for joy to surprise me takes more patience than I can muster. My own preference is to seek out joy, to chase it down, and to be constantly on the alert for humorous encounters with contagious joy gems. It's a deliberate decision I make every morning as I remind God of His joy-filled promises to me. Of course He doesn't need to hear these reminders, but sometimes I do!

Thank You, Lord, for this new day. You have said You will turn my wailing into dancing and You will clothe me with joy. You have promised to anoint me with the oil of joy, to fill my cup of joy to overflowing, and in all my troubles, to give me joy that knows no bounds.

Okay, Lord. I accept. Just lay the joy out there, dear Jesus, and I know I'll find it even if it takes some work, because Your joy is my strength, and I'm asking this in Your Name. Amen.[5]

For many of us, it *does* take work to find joy in the world around us. We have to keep *choosing* to look for it in unexpected places. Somewhere I read about an actress who constantly worked to make this choice. The article quoted actress Catherine Deneuve as saying she deliberately "cultivated pleasure because she wasn't naturally a happy person." The interviewer noted that "by taking pleasure seriously, she was able to reorient her inner compass and change her feelings, thoughts—and ultimately her entire mood."[6]

What a difference a happy, optimistic mood can make in our day, whether we're facing a classroom full of students, an office full of highly stressed coworkers, or another morning in the chemo room. One researcher called this way of deliberately choosing to be happy "learned optimism," and he found that "optimists better resist depression, infections and chronic diseases."[7] Having wrestled with a couple of chronic diseases, I'm all for finding *fun* ways to resist them!

The Joy of Jesus
Admittedly, it isn't always easy to discover the joy God has planted in each new day. It's like the little boy who eagerly dug into the big pile of manure, sure he would find a pony in there somewhere. When you're neck-deep in the cesspool, it's hard to appreciate all the fertilizer you're soaking up! But eventually, something silly lands in front of you, the laughter comes, and the next thing you know you're surrounded by a beautiful, well-fertilized garden.

An e-mail sent to me at the Women of Faith Web site expressed that idea this way:

> I have enjoyed laughing with you over many years, Barb. Now I am praying for you. Seek each day for the blessings of the moment. God sends so many "happies" throughout the day, even in the midst of chemo. He helps us wake up and become aware of them when we ask. That is my prayer for you: that God will heighten your awareness of His happies sent especially to you moment by moment.

Reading her note, I thought of a "happy" that had happened to me last year. I had gone to the beauty shop to get my hair trimmed (that, of course, was back when I had hair to trim!). The stylist had spread a big, plastic cape over me with another smaller white capelet underneath. The little cape looked like lace but it was actually plastic, too. When the stylist finished she removed the plastic cape and sent me on my way. I ran a few errands before heading home, and only as I completed my *last* stop did someone say to me, "Oh, are you going to a wedding?"

"Pardon me?" I asked.

The salesclerk reached up to my shoulder and fluffed the little white lacelike capelet that still covered my shoulders. The stylist had forgotten to remove it, and I had worn it in three different stores before someone finally asked me about it! Just thinking about that incident made me laugh all over again.

"Right Mr. Hanson—I have here the results of your tests . . ."

Cultivating Joy

When you deliberately cultivate a joyful outlook, it soon blossoms into an outward sign of your God-inspired character. You feel yourself filling up with the deep, fulfilling kind of joy Paul described as "the fruit of the Spirit" in Galatians 5:22. It's the kind of joy that begs to be shared. Surely that's why Jesus, as He commanded His disciples to "love each other as I have loved you,"[8] explained to them, "I have told you this so that my joy may be in you and that your joy may be complete."[9]

There it is in living proof: The joy of Jesus has already been planted in us. It's already there! And, believe me, Jesus' joy isn't a superficial or mindless thing. Instead, as one clergyman wrote, this kind of joy "is often sober, quiet and deep. It is not easily dislodged by passing moods or the ebb and flow of events. [It] conveys a sense of being firmly rooted in spite of—or even because of—the . . . difficult things that are woven into the fabric of our lives. Because joy is the work of the Spirit in us, it grounds us in the confidence, courage and consciousness of the risen Christ."[10]

This idea that Jesus has given us His joy came home to me when someone wrote to me:

> Barbara, thank you for your sense of humor, or maybe I should really thank the Father for that, for you certainly must have inherited it from Him! . . . Take care of yourself, keep laughing, and remember: It's not an apple a day that keeps that doctor away, it's laughter.

Another woman wrote:

> You are living proof that God has a sense of humor (take that any way you choose!).

Believe it: Jesus' joy is in me—and it's in you, too. Sometimes it just has to be fertilized and cultivated to get it to grow. And what blessings it brings when it sprouts!

Just thinking of that image of little seedlings of joy bursting forth from life's fertilizer reminds me of a funny note another friend tucked into a get-well card. She had read a little piece about all the skills mothers need, including the ability to cope with children who delight in stuffing objects up their noses. She wrote:

> I *did* stuff a bean up my nose as a child. It was a holiday weekend, and we couldn't find a doctor. By the time it was removed, the bean had actually *sprouted!!* Do you suppose I was trying to grow the beanstalk for Jack?

Unexpected Blessings

When I think of the blessings sprouting from unexpected places in our lives, I remember the conversation between two of Jesus' disciples. Jesus had called Philip to be one of His followers, and Philip wanted to share the experience with his friend Nathanael. He told Nathanael, "We have found the one Moses wrote about in the Law, and about whom the prophets also wrote—Jesus of Nazareth, the son of Joseph."

But Nathanael scoffed, "*Nazareth!* Can anything good come from there?"

Philip probably smiled confidently as he answered his friend: "Come and see."[11]

When Nathanael heard that the One promised by God had come from Nazareth, he couldn't believe his ears. You see, Nazareth wasn't exactly the Jews' idea of a nurturing, socially acceptable place that turned out social and cultural leaders of that day—certainly not the Messiah.

In the same way, when I was diagnosed with cancer, I got outrageous letters from women who assured me something good would come out of my having a malignant brain tumor. Many mentioned their own experiences in finding God's hope and goodness in the depths of their illnesses.

Cancer! I scoffed to myself as I read these letters, hearing the same tone rattle around my head that Nathanael must have used on that day so long ago. *Can anything good come from cancer?*

But the letters—so many of them!—helped me realize the answer is *Yes!* Here's just one example:

I, too, have cancer, and I have learned so much of God's provision and His nearness in my illness that I somehow feel almost blessed to have gone through it. (Of course, that is on the days when I feel good!)

Another friend pointed out,

"You can pretty much get away with saying anything. If it's inappropriate, people will just think it's the tumor, and you won't be held accountable."

Finding the Blessing in Everything

Each day the mail brings more notes sharing encouragement from all kinds of unexpected sources. One friend, acknowledging my nickname as the "Geranium Lady," sent a card containing a little vial of "body-soothing geranium oil."

Phew! I thought when I saw what it was. To be honest, I may be known as the Geranium Lady, but I sure don't like the way geraniums smell. Let's face it, the geranium has a bright, cheery blossom, but when it comes to scents, the poor geranium ranks right down there with stinkweed, if you ask me! But I read the card that accompanied the gift, and it insisted the oil would comfort, calm, refresh, quiet, and soothe me. So I opened the vial and took a little whiff. It was delightful! I could hardly believe my nose!

Then I looked at the rather long list of ingredients and saw that there was, indeed, some geranium oil in this little vial, but it was listed near the end, after aromatic emollients such as "sweet almond" and lavender oils. But that's so much like our lives, isn't it? If we only focus on the stinky stuff, it's easy to believe we're stuck in the manure pit. But if we put our difficulties in perspective, mixing together the hardships with all the blessings in our lives, we realize we're living in a garden of beautifully perfumed flowers—well-fertilized ones!

Thinking about that geranium oil brought to mind the comforting image from Psalm 23: "Thou anointest my head with oil; my cup runneth over." What an endearing image: the Shepherd's own soothing touch anointing my barbed-wired head with oil. Just picturing it, I feel my tension easing and my hair growing back! And then another phrase pops into my mind (as my friend said, I can ramble on this way now, because I have a brain tumor, you know, so I have an excuse). It's a thought from Emilie Barnes's book *My Cup Overflows with the Comfort of God's Love.* Emilie wrote, "It's a given . . . our cups will overflow with trouble. . . . But you and I could never know the wonderful things that God has in store for us when we bring him our overflowing cup of trouble, let him empty the pain, and then let him fill us to overflowing with his love."[12] And then, as the title of the old Jimmy Dean song says, "I'm drinking from the saucer 'cause my cup has overflowed!"

Finding something good in the troubles that find *us* can be an entertaining challenge. It's like searching the storm clouds for that rainbow when the sun comes out again. And even in the midst of the storm, there are blessings to be found. Recently I tore an advertisement for a specialized showerhead out of a magazine, just because I loved the message it shared. It bragged that this particular showerhead "washes away the stubbornest of bad days." The promised deluge, the ad said, "doesn't just wash away your cares. It drowns them!" What a different way of seeing a storm that sweeps over our lives!

About the time I was ripping that advertisement out of the magazine, I got a note from a woman who described all the problems she was having with her family. Then she said, "I take lots of showers, because that's the only place I can cry without being heard." Her words reminded me of that wisdom that says,

Tears are to the soul
As soap is to the body.

Our tears leave us feeling cleansed, even though they come from heartache. And when we manage to stop crying, we somehow feel refreshed and ready to take on the world again.

Finding God in the Fire
Just think of all the stories you've heard that describe something good coming from a bad experience, rewards arising from disappointment.

My dear friend Joyce Landorf Heatherley knows about reaping something good from a bad situation. In her book *Monday through Saturday*, which describes the chronic pain she suffered for many years, Joyce, who also fought against cancer, recalled a conversation she had with her sister while the sister was studying the Bible story of the Hebrew men who were thrown into the fiery furnace.

The story, told in Daniel 3, tells how the men were sentenced to death in the furnace by King Nebuchadnezzar after they refused to worship the king's golden idol. *The Living Bible* translation includes this stirring account:

> But suddenly, as he was watching, Nebuchadnezzar jumped up in amazement and exclaimed to his advisors, "Didn't we throw three men into the furnace?"
>
> "Yes," they said, "we did indeed, Your Majesty."
>
> "Well, look!" Nebuchadnezzar shouted. "I see *four* men, unbound, walking around in the fire and they aren't even hurt by the flames! And the fourth looks like a god!"

One day Joyce's sister called her excitedly, read her this passage, then paused and said to her, "Oh, Joyce, just think. The king would have *never* seen the Lord had the men not been in the furnace. Maybe the furnace of your pain is the only place others will really see Jesus. . . ."

The experience gave Joyce a "new appreciation of the furnace." She concluded that the "fiery experience is twofold: to refine us into the purest of gold and to let others catch their first (and possibly their only) look at Jesus."
Then she wrote this beautiful thought:

> *Real Christians*
> *know that sometimes*
> *the only way*
> *the world around us*
> *will ever see Christ*
> *is through the*
> *fiery flames of*
> *our own trials*
> *and suffering.*[13]

Believing that her pain created a new opportunity for witnessing gave Joyce the strength to carry on. "Maybe I can stay in the furnace a little longer. Are you game to stay too?"

ZIGGY   By Tom Wilson

Joyce's joy at being able to share her faith, even incidentally through her pain, mirrored my own feelings when I received this message from a woman in the Midwest:

For Valentine's Day my husband gave me a three-book volume of your books, and while reading it I have come to feel as if I know you personally. When I registered for the Chicago Women of Faith conference (my first one), I anticipated that hearing you in person and possibly meeting you would be one of the highlights for me.

Instead, to learn of your illness made the experience more real, sincere, or authentic. Instead of just a time to get away from it all, it became more worshipful for me. My "issues" were less important.

God does work in mysterious ways! He's touching many lives even through your illness and healing. May God heal you completely and restore you to sharing His Word and wonder. . . .

It's amazing to consider that just by being believers who cling to our faith despite an illness or a hardship, we might be able to encourage someone else. We might be, as the prophet Jeremiah wrote

. . . like trees replanted in Eden, putting down roots near the rivers—never a worry through the hottest of summer, never dropping a leaf, serene and calm through droughts, bearing fresh fruit every season.[14]

For me, this phenomenon is certainly a boomerang blessing if ever there was one, because *of course* I'm holding on to Jesus' robe tighter than ever right now.

There was a time in Jesus' ministry on earth when He confronted His followers, challenging them to believe what He had told them. Some of them couldn't handle the difficult lessons He was sharing. As a result, many of His followers left Him. Jesus, watching them go, turned to the twelve remaining disciples. "Do you want to leave, too?" He asked them.

I love the disciples' answer. It is the same statement that constantly fills my heart and mind, even when challenges beset me:

> Simon Peter answered him, "Lord, where would we go? *You* have the words that give eternal life."[15]

Who else would I cling to when my health fails or my heart breaks? Where else would I turn? Only Jesus offers glorious, eternal life. And to think that someone else could be encouraged by my own desperate death grip on Him is . . . well, just icing on the cake!

Delighting in Obstacles

Admittedly, I'm not the first one to experience this mystery. Another friend, Joni Eareckson Tada, wheelchair-bound for more than thirty years, is well acquainted with despair and disability. And she has seen how God has used her ordeal to show others the light of God's love. Instead of helplessly resigning herself to the limitations her condition brings, Joni has been inspired to write heart-stirring books and music, and she has painted beautiful works of art with a paintbrush grasped in her teeth. She also works through Joni and Friends, her worldwide ministry to the disabled. And today she says:

> Remember that you can learn to delight in every obstacle God places in your path. Limitations force us to yield, to abandon ourselves to our creator, God. And when we do, his creativity flows![16]

Then there was the apostle Paul, who, I suppose, could be called the poster child for Christians who suffer. His observation about this phenomenon of reaping blessings from something bad was translated in *The Message* this way:

I was given the gift of a handicap to keep me in constant touch with my limitations. Satan's angel did his best to get me down; what he in fact did was push me to my knees. No danger then of walking around high and mighty! At first I didn't think of it as a gift, and begged God to remove it. Three times I did that, and then he told me,

"My grace is enough; it's all you need.
My strength comes into its own in your weakness."

Once I heard that, I was glad to let it happen. I quit focusing on the handicap and began appreciating the gift. . . . Now I take limitations in stride and with good cheer. . . . I just let Christ take over! And so the weaker I get, the stronger I become.[17]

Whatever Your Situation . . . Choose Joy
Maybe it's not an illness you're facing. Perhaps it's a broken relationship, a bankruptcy, the loss of a loved one, or some other crisis when you find yourself sloshing through life's manure pit without any ponies in sight. Remember: In this life, pain is inevitable, but misery is optional! Purposefully *choose* to be joyful.

And do it with a smile. Recently I saw a magazine article that described a woman who infused her day with joy by singing or humming happy songs as the hours passed. She noted, "When folks sing about something happy, typically there's a smile in their voice."[18] And on their faces, I might add. It can bring a feeling of happiness even when you're not in a happy place.

My friend Lynda taught me that several months ago when a Women of Faith cruise followed right on the heels of the last conference of the year. We went right from one venue onto the ship, where a conference event was scheduled each day. It was fun, of course, but it was also exhausting to have to be on my best behavior for several days straight as I mingled with the conference attendees on the ship.

One morning, the thought of another long day of constant

interaction simply wore me out before I could even get out of bed and get dressed. Lynda, sharing my cabin, had just the remedy for me. She opened the sliding-glass door between our small cabin and the tiny balcony on the side of the ship and said, "Oh, Barb! The sun is coming up, and the waves are sparkling. It just makes me want to sing! Come out here and sing with me . . . please!"

Rather grumpily, I padded out to the balcony. The vast expanse of sparkly waves looked like a sea of transient diamonds. Lynda was already singing "When Morning Gilds the Skies." And it seemed perfectly natural to join in. We sat there, singing together—"When mirth for music longs, this is my song of songs: May Jesus Christ be praised!"—as the sun rose over the sea.[19] The experience was one I'll never forget. It was impossible to feel anything but joyful as our words of praise flowed out over the sea and God's beautiful blessings shone down on us.

The lesson I learned from that morning on the ship was . . . if you find it hard to be cheerful—fake it! Here's some how-to advice one writer offered:

Put on a happy face, and your body, either not knowing the difference or hoping for the best, responds as if the expression were genuine. The act of smiling engages at least three major muscle groups, increasing blood flow to the face and thus helping to create a rosy glow. Laugh heartily and you tone your facial muscles; get downright delirious and you get a serious aerobic workout. That soreness in your abdomen after a bout of hysterics means you've exercised those muscles. That pain in your backside probably means you laughed so hard you fell off your chair. You'll heal quickly, though: Laughter has a protective effect on the immune system by increasing antibody-producing cells and activating virus-fighting T cells.[20]

Whatever your situation, turn your self-centered focus off, turn your smile on, and look for the *good* that can be found in your circumstances. That's what Pam Costain did as she struggled to cope with a trying situation many baby-boomers face today. In a column she wrote for the Minneapolis *Star-Tribune*, Pam described how she found something good amidst the heartbreak of seeing her eighty-eight-year-old mother sink into the dark world of dementia. "Having my mother near me during this final period of her life has been a real blessing," wrote Pam, "but it has not been easy. In fact, much of the experience has been extraordinarily difficult."

Despite the difficulties, she wrote, "With each encounter I am challenged to be a better person—more compassionate, more loving and more giving. . . . When I take her out to sit in the sunshine or hold her hand when we visit, I am reminded of the meaning of the simplest gestures. . . . My mother's presence and vulnerability reminds my husband, children and me what it means to be a family. Every day we look into the fragility of human existence and can celebrate the simple things—love, compassion, trust, touch, surrender and gratitude."[21]

Whether we're dealing with a loved one's mortality—or our own—we can watch for opportunities to show love, joy, and hope. And by this sharing, we enrich our own lives. Henri J. M. Nouwen wrote that "joy and hope are never separate. I have never met a hopeful person who was depressed or a joyful person who had lost hope. . . . Joy is not the same as happiness. We can be unhappy about many things, but joy can still be there. . . . It is important to become aware that at every moment of our life we have an opportunity to choose joy."[22]

A Penchant for Joy
A friend in Florida sent me a newspaper clipping, saying she knew the name of the woman described in the article would make me laugh—and it did. But then I read the whole story and realized this woman had more than just a delightful name. She had a hope-filled mind and a penchant for joy.

The eighty-four-year-old woman was driving her little car down the Interstate in the middle of the night to pick up her granddaughter at the airport when she was rear-ended by another driver. Her car flipped over a concrete barrier and plunged into a mangrove swamp, hidden from sight of the emergency workers who searched for her for three and a half days. While she was stuck in the car, she prayed for rain. "When it came, she used a silver steering wheel cover to capture it and a pair of hospital bootie socks to soak it up and suck it," one newspaper reported. Her eventual rescue made headlines around the world.

Now, more than a year later, the woman still endures pain and nightmares related to her ordeal, but she doesn't let them get her down. "Life was meant to be lived and enjoyed, not to dwell on the bad things," she told the newspaper interviewer. What other kind of attitude could a woman have when her name is . . . *Tillie Tooter!* And wouldn't you know? She was driving a Toyota![23]

Tillie's troubles reminded me of some of my own driving challenges this year. Before one MRI, the technician injected some medication into my wrist. I guess my body didn't like whatever was injected, because by the time the MRI was over, my eyes had become so puffy I could hardly see to drive home. But as I drove, I thought of something funny, and that kept me going. That morning, as I had been leaving for the appointment, someone from the clinic had called, reminding me not to use deodorant or hairspray for the MRI.

"Hairspray!" I answered. "To use hairspray, I'd have to have hair!"

In Toyotas or Chariots, Ride Your Troubles to Heaven

Hannah Whitall Smith wrote that "earthly cares are . . . God's chariots, sent to take the soul to its high places of triumph. . . . When our eyes are thus opened, we shall see in all the events of life, whether great or small, whether joyful or sad, a 'chariot' for our souls. . . . Get into your chariot, then. Take each thing that is wrong in your lives as God's chariot for you . . . meant to carry you to a heavenly place of triumph. Shut out all the second causes and find the Lord in it. Say, 'Lord, ope my eyes that I may see, not the visible enemy, but thy unseen chariots of deliverance.'"[24]

Maybe your chariot of "earthly cares" is cancer or some other health problem. Or maybe you have a wayward child or an unfaithful spouse. Perhaps you're living in a high-pressure vise, sandwiched between young children who need your guidance and aging parents who need your care. Or maybe your life is on an even keel right now, and you're thinking none of this "in-all-things-be-joyful" talk applies to you. I smile as I think of you and recall David Jeremiah's words whenever he acknowledges that some people haven't endured any "disruptive moments" in their lives.

"Be patient," he says, always invoking laughter. "Just be patient. Those moments will come."

Moments of Mirth in the Manure Pile

Doctor to patient: "What you have is the common cold, and there is no known cure for it. But cheer up—it may turn into pneumonia, and we know what to do for that!"[25]

A father gave his little girl a puppy for her birthday. Just an hour later he found a puddle in the middle of the kitchen floor.

The man called out for his daughter, who came running into the kitchen and asked her to explain why she wasn't watching her new pet.

She looked at the puddle then looked up at her dad and said, "My pup runneth over."

Observation: Knees bent in prayer . . . don't shake.

Remember: A candle loses nothing by lighting another candle.
And blowing out another's candle will not make yours shine brighter.

MOTHER GOOSE AND GRIMM • By Mike Peters

© Tribune Media Services, Inc. All Rights Reserved. Reprinted with permission.

A woman went to see her physician, complaining, "Doctor, I don't know what to do. You've got to help me; I just can't remember anything. I've no memory at all. I hear something one minute, and the next minute I forget it. What should I do?"
The doctor replied, "Pay in advance!"[26]

We are most open to Jesus in the tough times of life.
The fertilizer of good soil never smells good.

—SOURCE UNKNOWN

During the last week in September, my phone rang incessantly with friends and acquaintances calling—to express their condolences. Several times as I picked up the receiver and said hello, I could hear the caller gasping in shock on the other end of the phone. "You're alive!" one person said, obviously dumbfounded.

The pieces of the mystery came together when a friend faxed me these two announcements in the Sunday bulletins from a local church:

September 23, 2001: "I had the opportunity to listen in on part of the funeral services for Barbara Johnson this past week. I rejoiced at the message of one speaker at her funeral: Because there is an empty tomb outside Jerusalem, I know that Barbara Johnson is alive today."

September 30, 2001: "Last week I mentioned the death of Barbara Johnson, and I must clear up which Barbara Johnson passed away. The Barbara Johnson who passed away was the Christian who was on the flight that crashed into the Pentagon on September 11th. The Barbara Johnson who speaks here every year and at the Women of Faith conference did not pass away."

We are pressed on every side by troubles, but not crushed and broken. We are perplexed because we don't know why things happen as they do, but we don't give up and quit. We are hunted down, but God never abandons us. We get knocked down, but we get up again and keep going. . . . Though our bodies are dying, our inner strength in the Lord is growing every day. These troubles and sufferings of ours are, after all, quite small and won't last very long. Yet this short time of distress will result in God's richest blessing upon us forever and ever! (2 Corinthians 4:8–9, 16–17 TLB)

Give me ambiguity . . .
or give me something else

What do you mean, it's not all about me?

One evening in early June, after I had completed the first three chemotherapy treatments and gone through another MRI, I received a phone call from my oncologist. Of the three specialists who were treating me, he was the one who had the most serious, no-nonsense disposition, and I felt intimidated by him. Maybe I was afraid I would burst out with some wisecrack and he wouldn't get the joke. Or maybe I was embarrassed to think he had opened up my brain and seen all my secrets. At any rate, when I heard his voice on the other end of the line, I was a little apprehensive, wondering why he had called.

"Mrs. Johnson," he said formally, "I have reviewed your latest test results."

"Uh-huh," I said, gripping the arm of my chair and preparing myself for whatever his next words would be.

"I see no activity in your brain."

No activity in my brain? Doesn't that mean I'm dead?

"Uh . . . n-no activity?" I stammered.

83

"That's right. We see no activity at all," the doctor answered in his quick, clipped style.

"W-well, w-w-what does that mean?" I was sure we were having a conversation. But if there was no activity in my brain then I must be dead, and if I were dead, how could I be talking? Why wasn't I being fitted for my new heavenly robe and stepping across the threshold of my new mansion?

"It means we've slowed the tumor," he said. Now I could hear the slightest hint of enthusiasm in his voice. "In fact, the tumor is regressing and resolving."

"Wow! For a minute there I thought you were telling me I was brain-dead," I confessed.

Finally he chuckled. "Oh, no! This is *good* news. Very good news," he assured me. Now his voice was taking on a warmer tone I'd not heard from him before. "In fact, it's such good news, I wonder if you might be willing to do us a favor."

"A favor? What could I possibly do for *you?*"

"Well, next Saturday is the regular meeting of the local cancer survivors organization. Would you come and speak to this group, give them a little encouragement? I know you're accustomed to speaking to large audiences all over the country, and this is a much smaller group. But I know they would benefit from what you have to say."

"I don't know . . ." I stalled, thinking of the fatigue that still filled my days following the chemotherapy treatments. "Isn't there someone else who could speak? There are so many others who have had more experience and who have more knowledge than I have about cancer. I'm so new at all this."

GARFIELD By Jim Davis

"No, there's no one else who can tell your story. I've read a couple of your books that you gave me, and I want them to hear you. If you can't come, we'll just have some members of the group take turns reading out of one of your books," he said.

"Well, I guess I could do it," I replied.

A few days later I was back in the chemo room, preparing for another treatment. Despite the hand-crocheted afghans that kept us cozy and the delicious cookies and lemonade the volunteers served, the place seemed forlorn. All the patients that day, with their slightly crooked wigs and out-of-season caps and head coverings, seemed quiet and the room somehow seemed sad. Before I sat down, I made the circuit of familiar faces, saying hello to the others already hooked up to their IVs.

"Are you chilly? I can get you another afghan," I offered to one woman.

"Ugh-gh-gh," she said in response, barely lifting her head.

"Could I fix the television for you?" I asked another lady who was staring off into space while a sports program blared on the tube.

"Ay-n't-care," she mumbled, shrugging and turning her head away.

Not knowing what she said but seeing she didn't want to talk, I moved on to the woman in the next chemo chair. "Would you like me to change the channel?"

"Ohhhhhhh," she sighed, opening her eyes briefly then closing them again.

"Good morning!" I said to the next woman, briefly touching the afghan covering her feet.

She only nodded in reply, smiling slightly.

As soon as I settled into my chair, the nurse came to get my treatment started. Watching her hang the IV bags and make sure the lines were clear, I marveled at the way this system worked. This was a toxic "cocktail," this combination of drugs flowing into my veins. And yet it was saving my life.

Soon a bit of nausea set in, and I struggled to push it back, mentally fighting off the churning stomach that settled over me like a cold, dank blanket of fog. As the poison dripped into my veins, all I could think was, *Whatever, Lord! Thank You, Lord. And, oh, help me, dear Jesus!*

Later that week, I attended a cancer support-group meeting, a weekly part of my schedule since cancer moved into my life. One woman in the group said her doctors had told her that chemo was her only hope—and she had been unable to tolerate the drugs. "I can't do the chemo," she said flatly, shaking her head slowly.

"What does that mean?" a member of the group asked her.

"It means I'm going to die," the woman said glumly.

Her words hung in the air a moment as we all sat there, a little shocked. Then I blurted out, "Well, heaven's looking pretty good to me right now, so that's not so bad!"

The woman smiled at me and nodded knowingly.

The Blessedness of Brokenness

Throughout the chemo treatments, my life had taken on a rather monotonous routine. I spent every waking hour at home, except for the required trips to the clinic. My other regular outing was to the nearby Drug Emporium pharmacy. Nearly every day I seemed to have some reason to pull on something to cover my head and drive off to that store. It was definitely time to break out of my rut. It was time to start reaching out instead of keeping myself bottled up with the feelings of fatigue. I was glad I had agreed to speak to the cancer survivors group.

Bill helped me put together a page of cartoons and jokes friends had sent me. We made several dozen photocopies of it on brightly colored paper, and I gathered up a couple of cartons of my books to give out at the "club meeting." We had fun, putting our plans in place. For a while, life almost seemed normal as we were once again planning a speaking engagement, complete with books and handouts.

When the day came, I wore a bright outfit, made sure my wig was on straight, and headed out the door with a spring in my step. Suddenly I realized how powerful the act of doing kindness can be. It felt so good to be on the *giving* end again

DILBERT

instead of the *receiving* end. Since my diagnosis, I had been flooded with so much kindness, myself, from cheery cards to tasty casseroles. It had felt really different to be the *recipient* instead of the *giver*. At first, I was uncomfortable with the whole thing, feeling I was somehow becoming beholden to these friends who reached out to me. Then, when I realized how ridiculous it was to let anything block the love that was pouring over me, I soaked up the care like a dry sponge dropped in water. The messages that were arriving in my mail became my daily vitamins. Here's a sampling:

> Barbara, you have blessed so many; now may you be blessed as the "many" let God speak to you through them. Hold on to that joy you've come to share. May there be many geraniums of love and faith in your hat this summer and fall as you rest and heal in the Father's arms.

> Barb, you have given so much to so many with your wit and humor—especially me. You helped me to learn to laugh again. May God bless you and keep you; may He wrap you in His arms and make you well.

> As you have helped bring healing in many lives with the writing of your books, your listening as people call you, and your writing to those in need, may these e-mails and cards you receive do the same for you.

"Thank you for calling the
Self-Esteem Center. You are wonderful
no matter how long we keep you on hold."

© 2002 Bunny Hoest. Reprinted courtesy of Bunny Hoest

Another day's mail brought a special gift from one of my Women of Faith friends, singer-extraordinaire Babbie Mason. She sent me a cassette on which she had recorded her song that I've often told her is my favorite. This time she sang it, on the cassette, just for me. The song was "I'll Be Standing in the Gap for You," and it expressed how she would be "calling out your name, praying for your strength." Just listening to it, I felt refreshed.

Then came another little gift in the mail that truly touched my heart. It was from Linda Hoffman of Rochester, New York. She had stopped by my book table at one of the Women of Faith conferences, hoping to get some of the little flat, shiny marbles I call splashes of joy. We used to give them out at the book table and urge women to put them on their sunny windowsills and let the sparkles remind them of all the places God wants to bless their lives. Linda had gotten one of the splashes the previous year and wanted to get more for her friends. She was shocked to hear my book-table helper tell her

I wasn't traveling with the tour due to my illness, that a videotape of my talk was being presented instead because I was still in recovery, and that we had discontinued handing out the little marbles in my absence.

Hearing this news, Linda's mouth dropped open in shock and tears filled her eyes. "Barb has cancer?" she asked, astonished. Suddenly she dug into the pocket of her slacks and pulled out a flat, shiny marble. "Barb's little splash of joy has blessed me so much, I gave it to someone else who was having a hard time. Then I started buying these smaller ones at the craft store and handing them out wherever I go. Please send this one to Barb and tell her that even though it's smaller than the one she gave me, it's sent with lots of love to bless *her*."

The little marble felt comforting as I held it in my hand and read my book-table helper's note, explaining how it had ended up in the packet she had sent. Just then the sun hit it, sending a sparkly beam of light bouncing off the surface, and I was truly blessed. Amazingly, Linda's gift was the first of several splashes of joy that arrived in packets sent after subsequent conferences.

One of them was the larger, sky-blue marble we had given out by the hundreds at the book table. A thoughtful woman had somehow had the marble engraved. Then, without leaving her name, she had dropped it off at the book table and asked that it be sent to me. When I pulled it out of that week's packet, my eyes filled with tears as I saw the single word engraved on the shiny surface. It just said, "Thanks!"

Another woman wrote to tell me she had carried her little splash of joy—she called it a pebble—with her as she was having medical tests, including a biopsy. "I held on to it to help me get through it all, and I want to thank you for that. Just keep thinking of all the pebbles in all the pockets of all those you've touched who care about you!" She signed her note, "A Pebble in Portland."

Thinking of all these messages that came my way, I understood that by gratefully accepting the outpouring of love, I was sharing a boomerang blessing—in a different-than-usual way. The givers were feeling the same blessings I had received over the years as I had enjoyed sharing the gift of joy God had given me. A friend described the situation exactly when she wrote:

> Barb, what a lovely thing God did in, yes, allowing you to endure one sad, terrible thing after another. You have been so faithful to Him that He, in turn, has allowed you to feel His love lavishly flowing through you to the world around you.

Try it, and you'll see what this friend expressed so perfectly. Even in your brokenness, in the midst of whatever hurtful experience you find yourself, reach out to help others, and you will, indeed, feel God's love flowing through you to bless another. You will become a *conduit* of His love.

Dubious Memberships

As we drove to the auditorium where I was going to speak for the cancer survivors, I marveled at how well I felt, how energized, when only a few days earlier the request to speak had seemed like another burden to be endured.

"I didn't want to be here today," I admitted to the group when it was my turn at the podium. "I never wanted to be in this cancer survivors group—never wanted to have cancer. But, then, I never wanted to be in Mothers Against Drunk Driving or to be in a group for parents of homosexual children. Also, I'm a member of a diabetes support group, which is so appropriately called Sweet Peas. I sure didn't plan on being in *that* group, either. For that matter, I never wanted to be in AARP! All these support groups are fabulous, but it's hard to think I'm qualified for membership when I never made application. But here I am, and I'm determined to let God use me here in whatever way He sees fit. I hope today He'll use me to give you some fun and, a little bit of encouragement. A long time ago, I said, 'Whatever, Lord,' and I still have to say it again almost every day. It's the prayer of relinquishment. I've relinquished my life to God, and He has given me challenges I never dreamed of. One of them just happens to be cancer."

The meeting went well, and I was blessed by the smiles on the faces of those who greeted me afterward with hugs and handshakes. Later that night, I was thinking about all the unexpected turns that have colored my life. I thought back on what life had been like *before* Bill's near-fatal accident, *before* our two sons were killed, *before* we learned that another son is homosexual, *before* diabetes and cancer became a part of the fabric of my life. Back then I had a normal life—happy, busy, simple, contented. And now, standing on the other side of all the heartaches, I know I would never *choose* to live through those experiences again. But I also know that my life today is a million times richer, deeper, more fulfilled than it ever was back then.

Sometimes I think of myself in my "former" life as simply a bystander, watching from the sidelines as others struggled through life-and-death situations. In that role, I was a little like Simon of Cyrene. He was standing on the streets of Jerusalem one day, two thousand years ago, when a commotion drew his attention. Suddenly a raucous crowd of soldiers and hecklers swirled down the narrow thoroughfare, and it must have taken a while before he could make out the focus of the ruckus. Then he saw a doomed man, obviously sentenced to crucifixion, struggling to drag a cross up the hill to the execution site.

Simon of Cyrene surely watched in horror as the man carrying the cross stumbled and fell beneath his burden. And then, probably before he knew what was happening, a soldier grabbed Simon from the sidelines and shoved *him* toward the center of the crowd. The next thing he knew, *he* was the one dragging the other man's cross up the hill.

The Gospel story doesn't tell us what happened to Simon of Cyrene after he was forced to carry Jesus' cross to Golgotha.[1] But we can't help but believe that his life was changed by his painful, humiliating experience when he heard what had happened to the One whose cross he had carried. Imagine how he must have felt when he heard the news that the man whose crucifixion he had been a part of had risen from the dead three days later! Remembering the weight of that cross on his shoulders, feeling the pain of the splinters that must have pierced his back, can't you just imagine how he marveled at the story he heard? And perhaps he believed, just a little bit, that without even wanting to he had somehow helped someone in need— and miraculously been blessed by the experience.

Sometimes I easily identify with old Simon. So many times I've been standing on life's sidelines when suddenly I'm swept into a hurtful situation not of my choosing. And somehow God has worked through each heartbreaking experience to create a blessing. It has happened so often that I've stopped being surprised by messages like this one, reminding me of the phenomenon:

> Through the Holy Spirit, you have allowed God to use you in so many awesome ways that I believe He will use you in whatever circumstances you are in (wherever, whenever, and *whatever*)! . . . I can't wait to see what God does in your life through *these* circumstances, Barb. You go, girlfriend! I'm watchin' you!

Passing on the Blessings

No matter what our circumstances are—and sometimes whether we intend it or not—we can encourage others. My friend Joyce called those who are deliberate encouragers "balcony people." They are the folks who perch in the balconies of our lives like proud parents, ready to applaud our every effort. As Joyce says, balcony people "love, listen, and care from the heart." They follow the "balcony motto" of 1 Corinthians 16:14: "Whatever you do, do it with kindness and love" (TLB).

Whatever you do . . .

. . . do it all for the glory of God.

. . . whether in word or deed, do it all in the name of the Lord Jesus, giving thanks to God the Father through him.

. . . work at it with all your heart, as working for the Lord, not for men.[2]

Commit whatever you do to the Lord, "and your plans will succeed"[3]—even if what you "do" is to show God's love as you suffer . . . or mourn . . . or face trying situations.

Whatever you do, you can still be an encourager, a balcony person for someone else, by the *way* in which you endure the hardship. In doing so, you will be blessed as well, as these letter-writers reminded me:

Barb, about eight years ago my father had lymphoma and went through a bone marrow transplant. His love for God grew so much during that time that he was able to encourage his doctors and so many other people who were ill. He is in remission and doing wonderful! Praise God! I know that God will use your experience, too, Barb, to be a light to someone else as well. Hang in there!

My mother is almost seventy and has raised five children of her own and five of her half brothers and sisters.

She took care of my dad for ten years when he had diabetes and heart disease, then she cared for her mother after she had a stroke. Now she is taking care of her fifty-year-old son who is suffering the effects of diabetes, kidney failure, and heart disease. I said all that to say this: She doesn't have a lot of upbeat circumstances in her life, but she still manages to be optimistic about life. During her very seldom quiet times, your books are such an inspiration to her to look at life with humor. So I pray that God blesses you back to good health, Barb, and that you have someone in your life to give you comfort and laughter during a difficult time.

Well, that lady's wish for me certainly came true. I've been blessed by the thoughtfulness of hundreds of balcony people who've reached out to bolster me during this difficult time.

My Favorite Gift
Of all the gifts that have come my way during this illness, my favorites are the cards and stories that have made me laugh. My friend Lynda, knowing my fondness for sending out silly cards, gave me a gift of thirty funny, *unsigned* cards and envelopes to send out to others while I was having the cocoon experience. Right away, I knew who to send them to. A friend of mine was going through a hard time, and I sent her one of the cards every day for thirty days. Sometimes, just for fun, I signed someone else's name—like Billy Graham or Barbra Streisand. Of course she recognized the handwriting and the postmark and knew exactly who was sending the zany notes, and that made it all the more fun.

In the most amazing demonstration of a boomerang blessing, as I was mailing out my one little encouraging card a day to my friend, dozens of cards and notes were filling my own mailbox. That overflowing mailbox was an apt illustration of the way God uses the simplest gesture to bless us as we help each other. Sometimes the notes I received were messages of thanks from women I didn't even know. Some

were notes of encouragement related to my situation. Others were simple snippets of silliness sent just for fun to share a laugh. I include some of them here, just to help you realize the wonderful gift a simple word of love or encouragement can be. So when you see something funny, snip it out and send it to a friend. Here's a sampling of the splashes of joy friends sent to keep me smiling as I fought the fight against cancer. I hope they inspire you to share something uplifting with someone you know who's stuck in life's manure pit:

You are such a blessing, Barb. No doubt you give God a chuckle a hundred times a day. Please get better as we women still have much to learn from you. We can't let you go home to heaven until all your giggles have been passed along to us youngsters. It is through laughter that we are reminded of hope.

I went through breast cancer recently, and I also had a lot of people praying for me. I used to think God was going to heal me just because He's so tired of hearing my name. I just wanted you to know one more sister is mentioning *your* name to our Father . . .

Having had some rough times in my health, I know that having a good attitude and sense of humor have helped me to find God in situations that I otherwise would have cried over. For example, I was in the hospital with clots in my legs that had thrown many, many smaller pulmonary embolisms, or bubbles, in my lungs. My hospital roommate, upon hearing of my condition, commented, "Boy, you sure are *bubbly!*"

Our ladies prayer group came to Nashville for the Women of Faith conference and went to the Rocky Top Saloon that morning for breakfast. No waitress was there when we arrived, but a couple of old men were *trying* to wait on several tables of ladies as well as four men at the bar who had already started their drinking day at 8 A.M. I decided to get up and help the two would-be waiters by taking orders. They were glad to get my help. In about five minutes, six other ladies started helping by taking orders, delivering food, cleaning tables, and even washing dishes. You should have seen those four men in the bar as they watched in amazement.

The waitress finally showed up and saw all of us working. As we left she said, "You may be the only Jesus these men ever see."

What a blessing to think how God used us Women of Faith ladies in the Rocky Top Saloon to share Jesus. What an awesome God we serve!

Barbara, you make me laugh and cry. I can only imagine that you are somehow finding ways to laugh and make others laugh during this challenging time. I'll bet you are curled up on Abba Father's lap, letting Him love you while discussing material for your next book.

Every time I hear the song "This Little Light of Mine," I think of you. We need to change your name from Barb to Beacon. You are a beacon of hope and joy to millions.

As you send out your own messages of hope and humor to friends in need of encouragement, I predict something wonderful will happen to you, as well as to the recipient of your greeting. It's a phenomenon described in Job 42:10, a passage my friend Joyce called "the last act in the drama of Job." It says, "Then, when Job prayed for his friends, the Lord restored his wealth and happiness" (TLB). Or, as the Geranium Lady might translate it, Job got a boomerang blessing!

Share Your Gifts
Perhaps you're thinking you just don't have the gift of encouragement. Well, think again! *All* of us were created to share God's gift of love with each other. It just takes some of us longer than others to discover the best way we can fulfill that assignment. When you're feeling insignificant and incapable, think of the Bible story of Gideon. When God told Gideon to "Go and save Israel from the Midianites! I am sending you!"[4] Gideon replied, "But Lord, how can I save Israel? My clan is the weakest in Manasseh, and I am the least in my family."[5]

Is that how you feel when you think of reaching out to share the joy of God's love with others? Do you think, *How can I reach out to someone else when I feel so miserable myself?* The Lord told Gideon, "Go in the strength you have. . . . I will be with you."[6] And that's what we have to do. We take whatever strength we have, and we use it for God.

Every Christian is blessed with plenty of godly love to share and a servant's heart for doling it out. How do I know? Because the Bible tells us we are made in God's own image. And Paul, writing to the Philippians, instructed them in Christlike servanthood:

> Love each other, be deep-spirited friends. . . . Put yourself aside, and help others get ahead. . . . Forget yourselves long enough to lend a helping hand.[7]

Paul told the Philippians their "attitude should be the same as that of Christ Jesus: Who . . . made himself nothing, taking the very nature of a *servant.*"[8]

As some of my letter-writers have reminded me, even when we're lying in hospital beds, we can *serve* the hospital workers with a smile and gracious words.

We can be watchful for any opportunities to laugh—and then share that laughter with those around us. As our strength grows, we can write notes of encouragement to others who are walking that valley of gloom behind us. That idea always reminds me of what Proverbs 25:25 says: "Like cold water to a weary soul is good news from a distant land." We can be as "good news from a distant land" by telephoning someone who's housebound and being a good listener.

Or we can offer to play the piano for a sing-along at the senior citizens center or bake cookies for the church bake sale.

Pat Swarthout is a volunteer cookie-caterer who enjoys sharing laughter as well as her homemade treats. When she was undergoing radiation for breast cancer, she made special goodies for the workers in the radiology center and became famous for her "love whopper" cookies that resemble little hamburgers. It's my kind of recipe: You don't even have to bake anything to make them! Just use yellow food coloring to turn vanilla frosting into bright yellow "mustard." Then toss shredded coconut with green food coloring to create the "lettuce." Now you're ready to assemble the "burgers." Two vanilla wafers become the "buns" and a Keebler mint cookie is the burger. Use the yellow-tinted "mustard" frosting to stick the ingredients together. Wherever you take them, you can bet faces are going to light up with laughter and anticipation as the sweet little "whoppers" make their appearance!

Now, maybe you're not a kitchen-based servant, like Pat is. But look around you. God has put something in your life with which you can show your servant heart. Maybe it's a sense of humor. Maybe it's a writing pen. One woman wrote to tell me when she had been very ill with liver disease a special friend from her Sunday school class sent her a note or card every week for all the many months of her illness. "What a special blessing those cards have been!" the woman wrote. In fact, they meant so much to her that she decorated her bedroom with them. "I've got every card anyone has sent to me up on the walls—new-fangled wallpaper!" she wrote. "Lying in bed just looking at them, what an encouragement it is. They stretch from my bed, around the corner, and about halfway down the next wall!"

Another woman wrote to say her mother had been murdered in a very high-profile case and she had been amazed to receive letters and cards from people she didn't even know. "It really hit me hard to know that complete strangers could have so much compassion for others. . . . It has truly inspired me to make certain that I pass along warm wishes when I feel them and not to just shrug them off."

Or maybe you can share another kind of "lift." Recently on a Sunday morning, as my friend Sue was ending a visit to Houston and being transported by a limo company from her hotel to the airport, she told the driver she was looking forward to getting home in time for church. The driver said, "I have one more fare after you, then we begin our Sunday morning limo ministry."

"Limo ministry?" asked Sue, perplexed.

The driver explained that she and another driver in their company, as well as two drivers from another limo company, take their limos every Sunday morning to one of Houston's homeless shelters. There they line up at the curb and welcome the homeless families into their sleek, luxurious stretch limos for the ride to a local nondenominational church.

"At first," the driver said, "some of the families came just to let their children ride in the limos. But the church service is so uplifting, they came back the next week for the blessing they received there. And we go into the service with them. Now it's like going to church with family. We get a blessing from it just as much as they do."

Maybe your reaching-out servanthood role can be simply visiting friends who need a cheery boost. You don't have to stay long (in fact, when I was housebound I appreciated the quick, ten-minute visits much more than those that stretched on for an hour or more). A short article in *Reader's Digest* shared how former Texas governor Ann Richards learned how meaningful such visits can be. During her mother's final illness, Ann "saw a dramatic change in her ailing parent" as the illness progressed. "After a lifetime obsessed with collecting cut glass, silver services, lace tablecloths, china and costume jewelry, her mother suddenly lost interest in her prized possessions. 'All that really mattered was who was coming to see her, her family and friends,'" Ann said.[9]

Or maybe you can serve others by simply sharing possessions you've been blessed with. In *Footprints of a Pilgrim*, Gigi Graham Tchividjian, daughter of Billy and Ruth Graham, tells the story of her parents' trip to the Congress of Itinerant Evangelists in Amsterdam. The international conference was attended by evangelists from around the world, including many impoverished preachers from Third World countries.

"On one of the last days of the conference, Mother was helping in the clothing room," Gigi wrote. "An African man came in looking for a dress for his wife. The clothing room had been pretty well picked over by this time, and there was not much left. After spending some time looking, this man could not find anything. Quickly, Mother went behind the curtain, took off her own dress, and, putting on whatever she could find to cover herself, gave it to this man to take home to his wife in Africa."[10]

There's no end to the kindnesses one person—or one company—can do with an attitude of servanthood. I love the idea a florist organization started called "Good Neighbor Day." On that day, participating flower shops give a dozen free flowers to any customers who bring a donation for the local food bank. The floral gift comes with a stipulation, however. The recipients are asked to keep one flower for themselves—and to give the others away to eleven other people.[11] Wouldn't that be fun to do?

The important thing is that word *do*. As my friend Joyce recalled, "It's funny, but when I was in mourning for our son, my grandfather, and my mother, I remember the *acts* of comfort by others . . . but I've forgotten all their words."[12]

Whenever You Can . . . *Do!*
Whenever you can, *do* something for *others*. Even when you don't feel quite up to it. Even when you've got valid excuses for not making the effort. *Do* it. Give it a try. And before you know it, you'll find yourself smiling and feeling uplifted. And don't make a big deal out of the kind deeds you do. Remember Jesus' instructions as relayed by Matthew: "When you do something for someone else, don't call attention to yourself. . . . When you help someone out, don't think about how it looks. Just do it—quietly and unobtrusively."[13]

The reward for doing quiet deeds of kindness are the words I long to hear as I enter those pearly gates. Jesus used them in a parable He told His disciples to teach them about using their resources wisely. He said, "Well done, thou good and faithful *servant*."[14] He didn't say, "Good job, *nurse!*" or "Great work, *Mr. Fix-it Man*," or "Way to go, *teacher*." He commended the character's servanthood, and that's what I want to focus on—both on serving others and in graciously accepting the help others express to me. There's a beautiful song that expresses our role as Christ's servants on earth:

> *Won't you let me be your servant;*
> *let me be as Christ to you;*

pray that I may have the grace
to let you be my servant, too.

I will weep when you are weeping;
when you laugh, I'll laugh with you.
I will share your joy and sorrow
'til we've seen this journey through.[15]

During my recovery, I've had to have several MRIs and brain scans. Usually the doctor's receptionist calls the day before the exam is scheduled. She reminds me of the time, and then she always says (as she did that first time), "Remember: Don't wear makeup and use no hairspray." And every time I think, *Hairspray? I don't have any hair! Why would I use hairspray?*

Then one day I was sitting close to the receptionist's desk as she was making her reminder calls. When she told one patient, "Remember: Don't use any hairspray," I had to laugh, because I knew the *man* she was calling. I had seen him, and he had absolutely *no* hair. On my way out that day, I heard her still calling patients and using these words. I stopped and told her it made me laugh.

She smiled. "Oh, I *know* most of the patients are bald. I say it even to the men when I know they're bald. It always seems to give everyone a little laugh. That's really why I do it."

Encouragement means to fill the heart, and that gal filled many bald-headed patients' hearts with her friendly calls.

Too Busy to Be Down
After my chemotherapy treatments were completed and I gradually resumed my work with Spatula Ministries, working on our newsletter, answering mail and phone calls, my cheerful attitude was restored. It felt so good to be *doing* something again for someone besides myself! Someone asked me then, "Are you depressed about having cancer?" and I could honestly answer, "No! I'm too busy." And just about that time, a letter-writer sent me a note that said, "Barb, you

remind me of Nehemiah when he was rebuilding the wall around Jerusalem. He said, 'I am doing a great work, so that I cannot come down.' Sounds like you, too, are doing a great work right where God planted you." And she was right. As long as I can function, I will refuse to let cancer—or anything else—pull me down.

Now, that's not to say I never shed a tear or felt a blue mood descending over me. In fact, when another friend asked me if I cried a lot during my treatment, I had to say yes. Every time I watched reruns of *Little House on the Prairie*, inevitably there were scenes that made me shed some tears—not for myself, though. I was usually crying over heart-touching trials that threatened Laura, Ma, and Pa. But the tears came, and I know it was one way of relieving some of the stress I was feeling about the whole cancer experience.

Tears can actually be refreshing, leaving us feeling cleansed and emptied of anguish. The important thing is to *stop* crying and *start* looking for ways we can reach out with our compassionate hearts to others who may need us. We feel better when we're doing for others. It's part of God's plan for us. Recently an item in the "Hints from Heloise" column noted that "feeling needed is the most important ingredient in being content." At centers for seniors or the disabled, "there is always a need for someone to gently guide a hand toward the target for the bead or yarn. Helping these people is the most rewarding endeavor imaginable."[16]

Now, it may be that you're not able to do anything physical for those around you, but that doesn't mean there's nothing you can do. As long as you're conscious, you can pray! I love this letter one lady sent me:

I have what I call "factory prayers." I work twelve-hour shifts at night. We are allowed to have radios at our machines . . . but sometimes I turn off the radio, and to the loud rumbles and hums and grinding of the machines I pray to Jesus for my family and me. . . . I like to think that God can hear me over the noise.

Another cancer patient wrote,

I have an encouragement ministry to help others who have pain or cancer, and I also have a ministry of prayer. Many nights I am awake with pain, but I just see that as an opportunity to pray for others. I am disabled, but that just gives me more time to pray!

A mother of three wrote to explain how a friend had inspired her to begin a "Blanket of Warmth" ministry. When one of her friends is ill, experiencing a loss, or "just plain hurting," this gal sends a warm blanket, along with an encouraging note and a poem she wrote. The poem concludes:

> *What a precious and wonderful gift*
> *We have in the Blanket of Warmth . . .*
> *Our Lord Jesus Christ.*[17]

From the Brokenness . . . Beauty
A beautiful example of how beauty can come from something bad was demonstrated by the members of a church that stands across the street from where the Murrah Federal Building was located in Oklahoma City. When the Women of Faith conference was in Oklahoma City, our sweet hostess took my helpers and me on a tour of the national memorial to those who died when the building was bombed in April 1995. While the memorial's many touching features made a profound impact on us, the thing that brought tears to my eyes was in the hostess's church across the street.

The First United Methodist Church suffered massive destruction in the explosion, and the church's elaborate, round, stained-glass windows were destroyed. But an amazing rebuilding campaign restored the structure while the congregation shared a building with another nearby church. And today new stained-glass windows adorn the front of the beloved old building. One of the beautiful windows is in the church's chapel. It was created from shards of stained glass retrieved from the original destroyed windows. The inscription worked into the breathtaking new window is a message of hope for all of us, no matter what tragedies we encounter in our lives. It says:

> The Lord takes broken pieces and
> by His love makes us whole.

No matter what tragedies you've encountered or mistakes you've committed in your life, God can use you to create something beautiful, broken though you may be. He can take the ragged pieces of your life and make you into a whole new creation that reaches out to others to pass along His empowering, restorative love. I'm living proof of that promise! And it thrills me to think others might see the messes I've been immersed in and be inspired to think perhaps they can survive their treks through the manure pile, too. I had to laugh when I saw the comment one Women of Faith attendee had written on her response card. It said, "I got to meet Barbara Johnson. She can be rather 'spicy,' which made me feel like there is hope for me!"

Jesus said we are the "salt of the earth"—and salt's a spice, isn't it? So let's sprinkle the earth with the love of God by sharing Christlike joy and kindness with others. And now, let's spice things up with a few laughs.

Moments of Mirth in the Manure Pile

A woman brought a litter of puppies to her veterinarian for shots and worming. The puppies all looked alike, and as they squirmed over and under each other in the box, the vet realized it would be nearly impossible to tell the treated ones from those yet to be treated.

So the vet turned on the water faucet, wet his fingers, and moistened each dog's little head when the shots and worming treatments were finished.

After the fourth puppy, the vet noticed that the usually talkative woman had grown silent.

As the vet sprinkled the last pup's head, the woman leaned forward and whispered, "I didn't know they had to be baptized, too."[18]

Try to name the five wealthiest people in the world. Name the last five winners of the Miss America competition. Name ten people who have won the Nobel or Pulitzer Prize.

Now, name three friends who have helped you through a difficult time. List the teachers who aided your journey through school. Think of a few people who have made you feel appreciated and special.

The people you'll never forget are not the ones with the most credentials, the most money, or the most awards. The people who make a difference in your life are the ones who care. And they will live forever.[19]

When a teacher asked her children what they were thankful for, one little boy replied, "I'm thankful for my glasses."

"Yes," responded the teacher, "so you can see better, right?"

"No," replied the lad. "They keep the boys from fighting with me and the girls from kissing me."[20]

Kindness is like softness.
It feels good to people.[21]

One of the most wonderful experiences of human feelings comes when we suddenly become aware that we are loved by someone else.[22]

One kind word can warm three winter months.[23]

Hospitality is making your guests feel at home—even if you wish they were.[24]

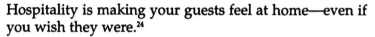

The best thing you can do for your heart
is to love somebody.[25]

Life is for service. We human beings are meant to be helpers. In fact, the greatest thing we can do in life is to help our neighbors come to know that they are lovable and capable of loving. Anyone who truly knows this will not lose hope.

—FRED ROGERS[26]

Lots of people want to ride with you in the limo, but what you want is someone who will take the bus with you when the limo breaks down.

—OPRAH WINFREY[27]

If you have much, give of your wealth;
if you have little, give of your heart.[28]

It is better to *give* than to *lend,*
and it costs about the same.[29]

"I THINK WE NEED TO START PUTTING SOME RESTRICTIONS ON THESE NON-CASH DONATIONS."

This most generous God who gives seed to the farmer that becomes bread for your meals is more than extravagant with you. He gives you something you can then give away, which grows into full-formed lives, robust in God, wealthy in every way, so that you can be generous in every way; producing with us great praise to God. (2 Corinthians 9:10–11 MSG)

Just think:
If it weren't for marriage,
men would go through life thinking
they had no faults at all

If you want breakfast in bed, sleep in the kitchen

Until I went through it myself, the word *chemotherapy* held no real meaning for me; I was completely ignorant of what it entailed and had no idea what would be required of me. When my oncologist described the rigorous routine I was to follow for the next several weeks, I was flabbergasted. He said for each chemo session I would come to the cancer clinic and spend several hours there in a big room with several other patients; like the others, I would sprawl there in a lay-back chair while a huge bag of liquid dripped into me.

Then, at home during the days preceding the chemo treatment, I would be following a very stringent schedule of taking six pills with thirteen ounces of water every three hours throughout the day and night. This procedure would be followed for four days prior to each treatment. The pills were not coated with that slick, sweet M&M surface that makes medications easy to swallow. Oh, no! These pills were dry and powdery and didn't go down easily at all. On top of all the pill taking and water drinking, I was supposed to relax and rest as much as possible, building up my strength for the next chemo treatment.

Being as undisciplined as I am, this complicated course of self-treatment was far beyond anything I could have managed by myself. But, as I mentioned earlier, I'm married to a navy man who *loves* being precise and dependable in everything from laundering socks (for years, back when *I* was doing the laundry, he stapled them together to ensure he got both of them back) to putting out the trash (he flattens the boxes and wraps up everything so carefully that on garbage-pickup day we're complimented on having the prettiest trash in the neighborhood). So when Bill heard what I was expected to do to prepare for the chemotherapy treatments, he took each directive to heart and made sure I followed the doctor's directions *exactly*.

To be honest, there were times when I got angry just hearing his cock-a-doodle-doo-o-o-o alarm clock go off in the middle of the night (the clock can play several other tunes, too, including "Oh, Susannah!" but "cock-a-doodle-doo" has always been Bill's favorite). Seeing him come my way carrying the glass of water and the muffin tin of pills, I was filled with dread. Now, looking back on those long, water-filled days and nights, I can see that helping me through that stressful period was probably like trying to help an injured dog. Sometimes you reach out to help the poor, suffering mutt, and instead of receiving your help gratefully, the dog growls and tries to bite you. Just picture yourself approaching a miserable, testy pit bull sprawled warily in a recliner or in bed, watching you testily and baring its teeth as you dutifully perform your loving act of kindness, and you have a picture of what it must have felt like to be Bill bringing me those pills many times a day.

But somehow we got through it, and when I was back in the doctor's office, once again complaining about how I detested all the water drinking and pill popping, the doctor was checking my vital signs and reading my chart. When we had both finished, he paused a moment, looked at me, and said, "Barbara, you have done amazingly well. You haven't missed a single dose of the medication. And it shows. You've responded wonderfully to the chemotherapy—and I think your progress is because of your husband's diligence in making you follow these procedures so accurately."

"Oh," I said, hanging my head and feeling guilty about all my whining.

Hotdog Blessings, Gemstone Goodness

When I got home, I told Bill what the doctor had said. Then I reminded him that his birthday was coming up, and I wanted to do something really special for him to celebrate the occasion—and to thank him for all that he had done for me.

"So . . . what would you like to do to celebrate? And what's a special gift I can get you to let you know how much I love you and appreciate you?"

He didn't even hesitate. "I'd like to go to Price Club and get a hotdog."

I should have known. For Bill, there are only two food groups: hotdogs and popcorn. And, being a connoisseur of hotdogs, Bill has decided the hotdogs served in the snack bar at Price Club are the world's best. So off we went to the big store.

Sharing our hotdog lunch in the cavernous building, I couldn't help but think how easy Bill is to love and how good he has been to me (not to mention how easy it is to shop for his birthday!). After I had finished my hotdog and was crumpling up the wrapper, my eye landed on my diamond ring, and I nearly got teary-eyed remembering how Bill had used the ring to give me a tender gift of love.

The ring was a gift from a neighbor lady of ours. When she died, she bequeathed several pieces of her beautiful jewelry to me; one of them was this large, two-carat diamond ring in a platinum setting. I enjoyed wearing it but sometimes felt a little ostentatious because diamonds are really not my "thing."

A few years later, we had a major financial problem, and I decided to sell the big diamond. The jeweler removed the gemstone and placed a zircon substitute in the platinum setting. No one ever noticed the difference, and I was content with the imitation jewels; after all, today's fake diamonds are very pretty, even though they're basically just glass.

A couple of years passed, and once when I had taken the ring off to clean it, I was admiring how good it looked, even though the diamond was a fake. Bill happened to be standing there as I polished it, and he said, "Here, give that to me. I'm going to take my ring to the jeweler to get it cleaned; I'll take yours too and have him give it a good cleaning."

Frankly, that sounded a bit odd to me, but, being an only child, Bill has always been a bit odd. So I gave him the ring, and he came back in an hour or so, smiling from ear to ear. He handed the ring to me and said, "It's real again."

"What do you mean, it's real?" I asked.

"It's a real diamond. A real blue-white diamond. I had the jeweler replace the fake one."

I stared at the large, sparkling, *true* diamond where the fake stone had been, wondering where on earth he got the funds to buy such a beautiful gem. Later I learned that for two years Bill had been saving part of his social security and pension checks until he had enough to replace the fake stone with a genuine, exquisite diamond. Now, every time I notice it there, sparkling brightly on my finger, I'm reminded not only of the kindly old woman who first gave it to me—but also of my kindhearted husband. Bill may have some odd ways at times, but some of them have been a real payoff for me. Like my diamond, he is the genuine article!

Adventures in Marriage

Over the years as I've spoken to audiences around the country, I've been accused of sometimes being a male-basher because I like to include in each of my books a chapter about the silly things men do. But having been married to a big teddy bear of a man for many years, I want to make it clear that I *love* men—especially Bill! But that doesn't mean I don't get enjoyment from the silly antics of the opposite sex.

In a magazine recently I saw a statement that said, "Marriage is a strange and necessary fire, a red-hot light toward which we moths cannot keep ourselves from flying. It's our source of pain and joy and transformation."[1] That last sentence certainly describes my marriage to Bill, especially in this battle against cancer. There's been some pain as we've watched each other reel from the dangers this disease holds for both of us. I've worried how Bill would manage without me if cancer becomes my ticket to heaven. And Bill has been tormented to see me suffer through the surgery and chemotherapy.

But there has been joy, too. With each batch of mail comes something funny we enjoy laughing about together. And throughout this ordeal, we've just enjoyed spending time together—a *lot* of time. In fact, my cancer was diagnosed in early March, and until mid-October Bill refused to leave me alone for more than an hour or so (while he ran to the post office to pick up the mail each day or stopped by the bank or ran other errands). He finally decided to give himself a break from Barb-sitting when our son Barney came down from Nevada and insisted Bill spend the afternoon with him on the golf course. And even then he made sure our other son, David, was "on call" and checking on me throughout the afternoon.

Frankly, I had really looked forward to having half a day all to myself. But as the hours drifted on, I found myself watching the clock and looking forward to Bill and Barney's return. It reminded me of another quote about marriage I'd read someplace: "The long, gray corridors of our daily lives are in fact blessed places where we can, if we try, find our true happiness."[2] In the long, gray corridor of my life, Bill—the one I jokingly call my joy-robber—has been a definite source of happiness for me. And his discipline saved my life.

Driving Each Other Crazy
So now that you know how much Bill means to me . . . let me tell you that despite all this closeness, we still have the ability

Bill has his cute little sports car for running all the routine errands. That's why he's known as "Gopher Bill" to our Spatula Ministries friends.

to drive each other crazy. And the craziest we drive each other is when we're actually *driving*. The truth is, we try to avoid driving each other anywhere at all! In my Ford Victoria, I'm as happy as a lark, heading off somewhere by myself to spread my joy. And Bill has his little sports car for running his daily errands; that's why he's known as "Gopher Bill" to our Spatula Ministries friends. Just last year he finally gave away his twenty-four-year-old Volvo for the last time. (We had given it away twice before, but like the dog in *Lassie, Come Home,* it kept coming back to us.) The car he drives now is just big enough for Bill and the mounds of mail he hauls to and from the post office.

So usually, when we're driving, we're by ourselves. It works out well, because there's no backseat driver to contend with, no one ready to point out our little quirks and errors. But sometimes, even when we think no one is looking, evidence of our occasional driving snafus leaks out. One day last year after Bill had been playing pool with his friends at the recreation hall in our mobile-home park, he came home and walked into my office with a disgusted look on his face.

"What's the matter?" I asked.

"Your name is posted three times on the neighborhood complaint board!" he fumed.

"What do you mean?" I asked. "I haven't done anything wrong."

"It's posted three times under the 'speeders' sign, right there for everyone to see," he said, shaking his head. "The guys were giving me a hard time about being married to a speed demon."

"Well, how fast did it say I was going?" I asked, still amazed.

"Twenty-five in a fifteen," he answered glumly.

"Twenty-five miles an hour is speeding?" I argued. "Who on earth goes fifteen miles an hour? *No one* drives fifteen miles an hour unless he's stopped!" Then curiosity got the best of me.

"Who else's name was on the board?" I asked.

"That's the worst part," Bill replied morosely. "The list just says, 'Barbara Johnson, Barbara Johnson, Barbara Johnson.' Apparently you're the only speeder in the park!"

I burst out laughing. It made my day to think of myself as a seventy-something chemo-induced speeder, *tearing* around the mobile-home park at twenty-five miles an hour! And I knew immediately which of my feisty friends had posted my name—I'm sure to give me something to laugh about. (But I have tried to slow down a little; I'm now topping out at about nineteen miles per hour.)

SIX CHIX

THE HAIRY ONES ARE FANTASTIC FOR BLOCKING DRAFTS.

BANNERMAN

Reprinted with special permission of King Features Syndicate

Marriage and Technology: a Dangerous Mix
Whether it's driving a car or operating new appliances in the home, implements of technology can easily become sources of

contention in marriages. I've already described what happened when I came home from the hospital to find that my laundry room had been converted to a space-age control center. I haven't done a load of laundry since then; Bill has been delighted to take charge of the washer and dryer cockpits—happily pushing buttons, turning knobs, and checking temperatures, just as he did in the days when he was a navy pilot.

Hearing him in there, humming to himself and enjoying the thrill of seeing stains disappear, I have to admit that occasionally I'm a little envious. During my many years of laundry duty, I enjoyed an occasional religious experience. For example, one day I took Bill's shirt out of the washer and was shocked to see that the whole front of it was stained bright red. It looked as though he had either been in a gun battle or had spent the day visiting a packing plant. Then I saw the candy wrapper in the bottom of the washer. Apparently he had left some red candy in his shirt pocket, and it had dissolved and turned the formerly white shirt into something a matador would wave in front of a bull.

The stain looked permanent to me, but I dosed it up with Zout stain remover and rewashed it in hot water, and when I lifted it out of the washer—it was as white as snow! That's when the religious experience occurred. Looking at that nice, white shirt and remembering how stained it had been, some beloved Bible verses came to mind:

> Though your sins are like scarlet, they shall be as white
> as snow; though they are red as crimson, they shall be
> like wool.[3]

If we confess our sins, he is faithful and just and will forgive us our sins and purify us from all unrighteousness.[4]

Yes, I enjoyed occasional moments of spiritual insight during my tour of laundry duty, but I'm happy to let Bill enjoy those special times now. He has always been one who loves technology, so the new electronic washer and dryer are right up his alley.

A Brand-New Day! (Not So Fast)
Last year, Bill tried to get me to make another (equally unsuccessful) shift into the high-tech era by convincing me to get rid of my four IBM Selectric typewriters and replace them with a new word processor. (We had four Selectrics, because, knowing I *loved* typing on them, whenever any of our friends moved on to computers they offered me their used Selectrics, and I happily accepted. Erma Bombeck also had four Selectrics, so I like to think I was just joining her in her writing method.) But the typewriters had begun to show their ages, and Bill was tired of hauling one after the other to the repair shop to have them fixed. So he finally convinced me to try a new word processor—an electronic machine with a memory and other amazing features. The momentous morning arrived when Bill loaded the typewriters into his car and disappeared out of the neighborhood. Filled with excitement (along with just a tiny morsel of apprehension), I watched him go then faxed a friend this note:

> THIS IS A NEW DAY! Today Bill is taking my FOUR IBM Selectrics to a guy and has ordered me a brand-new different kind—with a memory or something. I am saying good-bye to the machines that have typed all my books and newsletters for 20 years!!!!!!!! How I will miss them. But he is tired of taking them to be fixed. So next you hear from me will be on a BRAND-NEW lovely machine, which I will have to learn how to operate.

The reason I know what I wrote that day—March 10, 2000—is because my friend, knowing me all too well, *kept* the fax so we could laugh about it later. That time came the very next day, when I sent Bill packing off the "brand-new lovely machine" with orders not to come back until he had bought back my Selectrics from the typewriter shop! That day was my last foray into the high-tech era.

Soon afterward, my friend sent me a column written by a newspaper columnist who also had insisted on hanging on to his IBM typewriter. It sat on the desk next to his computer, and he vowed to keep it there "until it simply gives out. Then I'll put both of us out in the recycle bin. My guess is the folks driving the truck won't take either one of us."[5] My sentiments exactly!

I Want Things My Way
The older I get, the harder it is to make changes; I've lived long enough to know how things work best for me, and that's the way I want everything to operate: *my way*. Bill's more willing to try new things, especially if there are new buttons to push, new knobs to turn.

Our son Barney inherited Bill's fascination with gadgets and fixing things. He loved to take things apart and put them back together again—especially bikes. Unfortunately, Barney, as the youngest of our four sons, came at the end of a long succession of big brothers who tended to take after their mother in their harebrained mode of operation. They, too, liked to take things apart, but they just never got around to putting anything back together. And that included their dad's tools they had used to reduce whatever it was to a pile of nuts and bolts. By the time Barney came along, Bill had begun locking up his tools in a big chest in the garage so the boys couldn't get to them. He had had all he could take of opening the tool chest while he was hurrying to fix an overflowing commode or a broken chair or whatever and having his tools missing or scattered all over the boys' rooms or in the yard.

Then along came Barney, full of a longing to know how things worked and feeling that strange, male urge to take things apart and reassemble them. And there were Bill's tools, locked away inside the tool chest. It was a source of frustration for him, and by the time he was twelve, he had, in typical Bill Johnson fashion, figured out a way around the obstacle. Every day that summer, as soon as Bill left for work, Barney completely disassembled Bill's tool chest. He took the big doors off and helped himself to the tools he needed to work on his bikes. Then, before Bill got home, Barney would put the tools back right where he had found them, put the doors back on the tool chest, reinstall the hinges and latches, and plaster a look of innocence on his face.

One day, Bill opened the tool chest and found something missing. He was dumbfounded. He certainly knew *he*, being the eternal perfectionist, would never fail to return a tool to its exact and proper location. And he also knew he wore the key to the tool chest on his key ring that he took with him to work every day and that the chest had been locked when he opened it. So what was going on?

Finally, Barney had to confess what he'd been doing. He had evidently forgotten to put away one of the tools when he had reassembled the tool chest that day. So the secret was out. Seeing the look on Barney's face as he sheepishly admitted his "crime," I was reminded of that Bible verse that says, "He who conceals his sins does not prosper, but whoever confesses and renounces them finds mercy."[6]

Bill was incredulous when Barney "confessed his sin" and admitted that he'd been regularly using Bill's tools all summer. As he demonstrated to Bill how he had taken the doors off the tool chest every day and then carefully put them back on, Bill was obviously awash with many conflicting emotions. Of course he was angry that, once again, one of his sons had borrowed one of his beloved tools and failed to return it. And he was a little embarrassed to be outfoxed by a twelve-year-old mechanic. But the hardest thing to admit was probably that he was proud of his son for being so smart and so talented!

Returning to What's Important
Remembering the full range of emotions Bill showed as he comprehended Barney's latest escapade, I realize I've felt the same range of emotions about myself and our marriage as I've gone through the cancer experience. There's been frustration

because cancer interrupted my plans and also because Bill has been so insistent that I follow the chemotherapy protocol precisely. There's been amazement in seeing how my body responds positively to this regimen of poison. And there's been a sense of pride in seeing that, as hard as it's been, we've survived this hurdle in our lives and in our marriage.

As many of my friends and family members often remind me, I'm a very independent person who likes to get up and go, go, go. Instead, during these past few months I've known fatigue like nothing I've ever experienced, and at times that has made me almost totally dependent on Bill for everything from housekeeping to phone answering, which he *never* did before. In fact, when one of my friends called and Bill answered, she nearly burst into tears, sure that I had died. She figured if Bill was answering the phone, something drastic had happened!

It hasn't been easy. Bill and I are pretty cemented in our ways. And yet there have been abounding blessings in this time of change. As much as I've loved Bill for all these years, I now have an even greater appreciation for all he has done to keep our marriage—and *me*—going. I've heard from many other wives who've described how their husbands have stepped into the turmoil left in the wake of the wife's illness or disability to do jobs they never thought they'd have to do. Usually it's the wives who write to tell me about these experiences. But one of the messages was from a man. He wrote:

> My name is Bob. I married a Barbara. Our last name is Hannah. We sometimes tell friends that our children are "Hannah-Barbara" productions. Did you smile? I hope so! You see, my Barbara has been diagnosed with fibromyalgia, which disables her at times. One of the encouraging things I have done for her is to give her some of your books and calendars. It goes a long way in helping her.
>
> Of her many talents, she is an RN, but she has not been able to do this occupation and instead has become our family's homeschool wonder-woman. It seems at times when we are unable to do the tasks we are accustomed to doing, God provides a way and gives us strength to do other work. I do hope in your recovery time you find strength and are able to do His work as it appears to you.

This man's sweet attitude and loving words for his wife make me think he has his priorities straight. He obviously cherishes his wife and their children—and wants to let the world know! Sometimes we come to that point easily. But other times, it takes an illness or another family crisis to help us realize what's really important. Those with high-powered careers sometimes have the hardest time making their faith and their family relationships a priority. The fortunate ones get a wake-up call before it's too late. One movie star recently admitted to *Parade* magazine that his success had blinded him

My dreams have been to get the "Super career" instead of focusing on)Gods plan for me to what was most important. "When you're living in the fast lane, you tend to overlook the basic components that give your life meaning—relationships, getting to know someone really well, putting someone else first," he said. "People who are highly ambitious often don't focus on the needs of their immediate family."[7]

Of course, there are also those of us who feel like the woman who said, "I want to live in the fast lane . . . but I'm married to a speed bump!"

BLONDIE By Dean Young and Denis Lebrun

Reprinted with special permission of King Features Syndicate.

The Best Form of Communication
One of the best things husbands and wives can do together—in sickness and in health—is to laugh together. Last year a woman who had attended a Women of Faith conference had spotted Bill sitting in the audience when it was my turn to speak. Later she wrote to me:

> Just one thing I'd like to share—how your husband can still laugh when he listens to you speaking at the conference, even though he has heard the stories so many times. I found that delightful! God's healing presence is obviously all around you.

Now, what this gal might not have been able to see is that Bill's eyes could have been glazed over and he was smiling in his sleep! Or he might have been laughing because he realized I had forgotten a line and was desperately trying to cover my mistake and instead was digging myself deeper into a hole. Or he might have discerned that I was having trouble with my microphone. As speakers, we wear a battery pack and a headset microphone, and ideally the battery pack is clipped to a belt. But frankly, I'm an *elastic* kind of woman rather than the belt-wearing type. And sometimes when the elastic in my slacks is a little stretched out, the weight of the battery pack pulls at my waistband. As a result, there have been moments when I'm standing on stage in front of twenty thousand women and I start to feel my slacks going south!

Obviously, this sensation is a little distracting, and as I continue speaking while at the same time I'm doing a (hopefully) discreet squirm-twist-and-pull routine to keep my slacks up, those who know me well can tell that something's amiss. They're usually the ones in the audience who are laughing the hardest! And of course, Bill knows me best . . .

It's great when two people know each other well enough to read the hidden meanings in those little secret signals we give

NON SEQUITUR By Wiley

off from time to time. And it's an even better thing when we can teach our children to be equally perceptive. I chuckled last year at an article someone sent me titled "Recipes for Life." It included newspaper readers' favorite tips about marriage they had learned from their mothers. The most practical tip was this: "Always set the table first. That way it looks as though something is going to happen, even though you haven't begun to prepare dinner yet!" And the most romantic tip was about one of those little hidden-message communications. This *ninety*-year-old mother told her daughter, "If you're cooking dinner and your husband comes up behind you and nuzzles your neck, turn off the stove. He's not that hungry anyway."[8]

Psychologist John Gottman says how we respond to each other's "bids" for communication—whether it's simply a routine "how-was-your-day?" greeting or an unexpected neck-nuzzle in the kitchen—is important to keeping the connection strong. We have a choice in how we respond to these bids for communication. By the way we respond, we either turn toward the spouse or we turn away. The key, says Gottman, is to be aware of the opportunity to connect.

"People can learn to become more open and responsive to their partner's bids as well as how to make bids that invite responses," Gottman said. "It's about awareness. . . . When people turn away, it's almost never mean-spirited; it's just thoughtless." Questions like "What do you like about . . . ?" are "bids" that invite a connection, he says. And the more such connections we have, the greater the reservoir of good feelings we share to draw on throughout our marriage.[9]

Of course, it's just not possible for all husbands and wives to be on the same wavelength and be responsive to each other all the time. Bill and I are well-acquainted with that scenario, too. One time last year we were coming home from the doctor's office, and we were both distracted by feelings on opposite ends of the spectrum. Usually I prefer to go to my appointments alone, because Bill gets impatient in doctor's office waiting rooms, and his fuming makes me start fidgeting, too. But that day he went with me, and the doctor's report was good.

We walked outside, and the sun was shining in a rare, smog-free Southern California afternoon that was simply gorgeous. The day was so beautiful that I just had to stop a moment and breathe in the sweet air of life. Bill, of course, was intent on finding the car and getting out of the parking lot ahead of any other drivers who might be heading for the exit.

As I slid into the car seat, I heaved a happy sigh and said, "You know, Bill, every once in a while, there's one little transient moment when I think everything's going to work out, and I just feel myself filling up with joy." I turned to him with my brightest smile and said, "Do you ever have those moments?"

"Yeah," he said, slamming the car door and then rolling down the windows while looking around for the nearest exit.

I sighed again, obviously *alone* with my thoughts. Not too long afterward, someone sent me an article headlined "Study: Men use only half of brain to listen."[10] *Amen,* I thought when I read it.

HAGAR THE HORRIBLE • By Chris Browne

Reprinted with special permission of King Features Syndicate

A Man Made Mute

One of the most remarkable Bible stories about communication between husbands and wives is the funny thing that happened to Zachariah when he heard that his wife was pregnant. (Well, *I* think it's funny; Zachariah might have disagreed.) The story, as told in *The Message* translation of Luke 1, says Zachariah and his wife, Elizabeth, "lived honorably before God, careful in keeping to the ways of the commandments and enjoying a clear conscience before God. But they were childless because Elizabeth could never conceive, and now they were quite old."[11]

Then one day while Zachariah was working in the temple, preparing for "his one turn in life to enter the sanctuary of God and burn incense," an angel suddenly appeared. The angel told Zachariah, "Elizabeth, your wife, will bear a son by you. You are to name him John. . . . You're going to leap like a gazelle for joy."

Zachariah, perhaps distracted by his impending duties in the temple's important religious ceremonies, reminded me of Bill's distracted "Yeah" that day when I was suddenly filled with a sense of well-being. He said impatiently to the angel, "Do you expect me to believe this? I'm an old man and my wife is an old woman."

The angel replied, "I am Gabriel, . . . sent to bring you this glad news. But because you won't believe me, you'll be unable to say a word until the day of your son's birth."

The next thing he knew, Zachariah was standing before the congregation, unable to speak. It was his big day, and he had to use sign language to get his message across!

We just have to laugh, imagining the sign language Zachariah must have used when he went home and *silently* tried to tell Elizabeth she was about to become pregnant and that he'd seen an angel and been struck mute! Just thinking about Bill coming home and playing charades to deliver such a message to me at our age sends me into gales of laughter! I'm sure the harder Elizabeth tried to understand, the more perplexed she became. Perhaps the harder Zachariah worked to convey the message, the harder Elizabeth laughed at his antics. I imagine her finally patting his weary shoulders and leading him off to bed to rest . . .

At any rate, their son, John (who would become John the Baptist), was born nine months later. Their friends and family expected the couple to name the baby after his father. But Zachariah adamantly (and still silently) refused. He finally found a slate and wrote, "His name is to be John." And that did the trick. Suddenly he could speak again—and what a story he had to tell! The Bible doesn't draw this conclusion anywhere, but I have a feeling after this experience that old Zach became a much better listener!

JEFF MACNELLY'S SHOE   Chris Cassatt and Gary Brookins

© Tribune Media Services, Inc All Rights Reserved Reprinted with permission

Mischief in the Classroom

It's part of my quirky character to enjoy poking fun at men every chance I get—especially when the men involved are kind-hearted gentlemen who also enjoy a good laugh now and then. My most recent escapade came about when a friend of mine relayed a seminary instructor's words encouraging his students to focus on the Bible and other classics of Christian literature, which is, of course, very good advice. Then he said, "The problem with too many Christians today is that they only read the fun books that are like candy or sugary frosting—books like *Stick a Geranium in Your Hat*. I have nothing against candy, but I think it's a big problem when that's *all* a person eats."

Well, the remark got back to me, of course, via one of the students in the class, and the more I asked about this seminary instructor, the more I thought he sounded like someone who could take a joke. So I asked the friend if it might be possible to visit the class sometime soon. Without telling the teacher who was coming, he asked if he could bring a guest, and the teacher agreed. What fun it was for my friend Lynda and me to plan our mischief! We set up a date to come, and I ordered enough copies of my book *Stick a Geranium in Your Hat and Be Happy!* for each student in the class (and the instructor) to have one. Then we bought a large red geranium plant as well as cupcakes with lots of *fluffy, sugary* frosting, packed a Precious Moments "Barbara" doll, and set off for campus.

Lynda and I left the cupcakes and books hidden around the corner down the hallway as we settled into the desk-chairs in the classroom. As soon as the class started, we knew we were *way* out of our league. Did I mention the name of the class? His-torical Theology Survey. And the class was *three hours long*. If I hadn't been so keyed up with anticipation, I probably would have dozed off and fallen right out of my seat. Fortunately, the merciful instructor, Dr. Alan Gomes, announced midway through the session that we would take a break and "meet our visitors." That's when our student friend stood up and introduced us.

Dr. Gomes's face changed from polite indulgence to beet-red embarrassment when he realized I was the author of *Stick a Geranium in Your Hat and Be Happy!*—and that he'd been had. But he was such a good sport about the whole silly affair. We served up the cupcakes and passed out the books, and he invited me to talk to the students. Standing in front of the class, I admitted to them that it *was* a ridiculous title, and com-pared to the classics of Christian literature it was definitely a lightweight. On the other hand, I said, it was obvious that God had blessed the story I shared in the book, because it has sold a million copies, had remained on the bestseller list for eigh-teen months after it was published, and everywhere we go with the Women of Faith conferences, women tell me it made a difference in their lives.

"You travel with the Women of Faith conference?" Dr. Gomes asked.

"Yes, I'm one of the speakers," I answered. "I haven't been traveling recently due to the cancer, but the conference plays a videotape of my talk."

Dr. Gomes's mouth fell open. "My wife isn't going to believe this! She just went to the conference in Anaheim and loved it!" Then he paused.

"You know," he continued, "I hope that the comment I made to my class about your book didn't hurt your feelings."

"Oh, you didn't hurt my feelings," I laughingly assured him. "It's been such fun to come here today and get to share my joy. We thank you for letting us play this joke on you." Then I handed him the perky little doll to take home to his wife.

"You're probably going to put this in your next book, aren't you?" he continued, looking worried.

"Of course!" I laughed.

"I just hope you don't make me look like too much of a nerd," he said.

"Don't worry," I assured him. "It'll be fun for both of us."

Thank you, Dr. Gomes, for letting me intrude into your scholarly classroom with my ridiculous goofiness. During my adventure with cancer, I didn't get out much. That foray of frivolity into your academic world was one of the highlights of that stressful time. And somehow, I don't think I would ever have had the nerve to do it if the class had been taught by a woman!

Dr. Alan Gomes was a good sport when I threw a surprise party for him and his students in his classroom at Talbot School of Theology.

Moments of Mirth in the Manure Pile

Q. How would you make a marriage work?
A. Tell your wife she looks pretty even if she looks like a truck.

—RICKY, AGE TEN

A pastor and his family had a kitten that climbed a tree and couldn't get down. The pastor coaxed, offered warm milk, and did everything he could think of, but the kitten would not come down. The tree was tall but not sturdy enough to climb. So the pastor lassoed the top of the tree with a rope and tied the other end to his car; then he eased the car down the driveway, hoping to pull the treetop down so he could reach the kitten. But just as he got the tree bent low and was climbing out of the car, the rope broke. The tree "boinged" and the kitten went sailing through the air—out of sight.

The pastor felt terrible. He walked all over the neighborhood asking people if they'd seen a little kitten. No. Nobody had seen a stray kitten.

So he prayed, "Lord, I commit that little kitten to Your keeping," and went on about his business.

A few days later he was at the grocery store and met one of his church members—a known cat-hater. He was amazed to see cat food in her shopping cart.

"Why are you buying cat food when you hate cats so much?" he asked.

"You won't believe this," she said. She told him her little girl had been begging for a cat but she kept refusing. Then a few days earlier, the child had begged again, and the mom finally said, "Well, if God gives you a cat, I'll let you keep it."

She told the pastor, "I watched my child go out in the

yard, get on her knees, and ask God for a cat. And really, Pastor, you won't believe this, but I saw it with my own eyes. A kitten suddenly came flying out of the blue sky, its paws outspread, and landed right in front of her!"[12]

Never criticize your spouse's faults;
if it weren't for them, your mate might have
found someone better than you.[13]

"I'll be away on business for a few days. So while I'm gone, you're the man of the house. Here's the remote."

A few years ago, a joke was making the rounds, speculating on what would have happened if the three wise men had been three wise *women:* They would have asked for directions, arrived on time, helped deliver the baby, cleaned the stable, made a casserole, and brought *practical* gifts.

When the joke appeared in the "Dear Abby" column, Lloyd and Kathy Rappleye countered with this argument:

"The problem with the joke is that the three wise men *did* ask for directions. As a result, Herod was tipped off to the birth of the Messiah, necessitating the flight of Mary, Joseph and the baby Jesus to Egypt. It also caused the deaths of thousands of innocent children. Little wonder that men have been afraid to ask for directions ever since."[14]

Another jokester speculated about what would have been said *after* the three wise women left the stable:

"That baby doesn't look anything like Joseph!"

"Can you believe they let all those disgusting animals in there!"

"And that donkey they were riding has seen better days, too!"

"Want to bet on how long it will take until you get your casserole dish back?"[15]

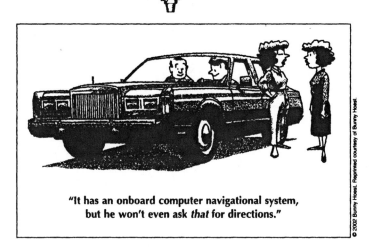

"It has an onboard computer navigational system, but he won't even ask *that* for directions."

For you were once darkness, but now you are light in the Lord. (Ephesians 5:8)

Everything is okay in the end. If it's not okay, then it's not the end!

Even when you fall flat on your face, you're still moving forward

during my months of treatment, when I had doctor's appointments every week and frequent tests and regular chemotherapy sessions, there always came a moment near the end of each doctor's visit when I would hold my breath and pray a silent prayer: *Please, Lord, don't let him reach for the prescription pad. And please don't let him order more tests.*

But of course God and the physician, knowing what they were doing, often had other plans for me. So quite often, a new medication was prescribed, one that might send me stumbling off into la-la land or cause my body to swell up like a watermelon. Or a new test or scan was ordered.

"All these tests," I muttered one day as the doctor was writing out yet another order for yet another test. "I detest these tests! When am I going to *graduate* from all this testing?"

The question probably popped out because I'd heard a dad say the same thing recently in our support group for hurting parents. "Doesn't anyone ever *graduate* from this support group?" he had asked wearily. We all laughed when he said it, because it seemed whenever we parents got through one crisis with our adult children, another horrendous problem would crop up.

The doctor responded to my question the same way we had responded at our support group. He chuckled, then he drew in a breath and said, "Barb, we're not seeing any signs of the tumor in your brain. We think it's gone. It looks like you're in remission. So yes, you might consider yourself 'graduated' from this problem . . ."

That next word was there, waiting to be said. It was the word *but* . . .

"But being in remission doesn't mean you're cured," he continued. "I'm sorry to say, this type of cancer is a kind that sometimes comes back. So we have to remain vigilant, and we have to keep doing tests. Because if it does come back, we want to attack it again right away and stay ahead of it. You're going to need an MRI every month or so to monitor your health."

Every month . . . He almost sounded like a judge, passing sentence on me. On the drive home, that thought persisted, and it reminded me of a belief that's often erroneously linked to suffering. Sometimes we're tempted to see our sickness as a punishment from God for our human failures. But it's just not true. Human heartache is not God's way of punishing us. In fact, making such statements to those who are hurting is nothing short of "ambush theology" that contradicts what Jesus Himself said while He was on earth. When Jesus and His disciples encountered a man who had been blind since birth, the disciples asked Jesus, "Who sinned, this man or his parents, that he was born blind?"

Jesus' answer is still reassuring today to all of us who long to see His goodness brought forth from our suffering. He said, "Neither this man nor his parents sinned, but this happened so that the work of God might be displayed in his life."[1]

John 9:1-3

re is a reason I am unemployed—
wants me to draw closer to Him.

"Dad said you got a 24-hour virus . . . How much time do you have left?"

God's Glory Revealed

Did you get that? Health problems and heartache aren't God's punishment for sin. In fact, they are just the opposite— a way for God to display His glory. I'm living proof of that. God's glory has been revealed in my life as He has healed my broken heart and sustained me through many other challenges, including diabetes and cancer. As someone once said,

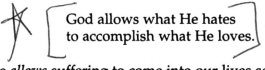

> God allows what He hates
> to accomplish what He loves.

He *allows* suffering to come into our lives so that His glory can be revealed in us. He doesn't send it, but it comes to us through His filter. As harsh as life's trials can be, it thrills me to think that somehow my suffering might be used to accomplish God's glorious purpose somewhere, somehow. In fact, the apostle Peter wrote that in suffering we are following Christ's example: "To this you were called, because Christ suffered for you, leaving you an example, that you should follow in his steps."[2]

We live in an imperfect world where pockets of chaos exist —chaos like cancer and the death of loved ones and other painful experiences. God brings us through these crises and makes us stronger in the broken places. With His help, much good can come from our trials. Even great personal loss can be redemptive when it leads us to feel deeper compassion and richer humanity.

When healing comes or when the heartache eases, we rejoice. Sometimes it happens through miraculous cures; sometimes it's through the work of doctors, scientists, and others in the healing community. And sometimes healing doesn't quite come. Sometimes instead we land in a place called "remission."

NON SEQUITUR   By Wiley

NON SEQUITUR © 2001 Wiley Miller. Dist. By UNIVERSAL PRESS SYNDICATE. Reprinted with permission. All rights reserved.

Living on the Edge

As I write this, I am still in remission. The cancer is gone but not cured—invisible but perhaps hiding. It's been a few weeks now since the doctors announced my new status, and I've found there is an edge to living in remission. At first, I was surprised that I didn't feel relieved. In fact, I was disappointed because the doctors didn't tell me the disease was completely eradicated; instead they said it had "regressed." Knowing it might still be lurking, undetected, somewhere in my body, I felt anxious. To be honest, it felt like a time bomb might be ticking inside me that might explode at any time.

Meanwhile, my friends and family wanted to celebrate the occasion—celebrate that the treatment was finished and that the cancer is gone. But I could not let go of my constant awareness that at any time this ugly disease might reawaken inside me. As a result, I sometimes felt reluctant to talk honestly with friends for fear of depressing them and dampening their happy feelings, even though it is usually good to talk because it helps me vent and it gives them a better understanding of what this illness feels like from my point of view.

It is painful to live with this kind of uncertainty, but I know the whole world right now is full of similar feelings, unsure what the future holds. We all know that at any moment an ugly monster of pain might reawaken somewhere and send us all into chaos. So perhaps we all share many of the same feelings these days. Maybe we're fearful of making long-range plans. Maybe we worry our loved ones will become impatient about our anxiety and will distance themselves from us to further avoid the emotional distress that comes from being around us.

Ah, stress! Without it we would just be a band of stretched-out elastic, and our feelings would fall flat on the floor!

Unexpectedly Lonely
When you're in the middle of a major illness, you think, *When I get well, my life will be normal again.* You think "normal" will happen automatically when your health is restored. But there's an emotional transition between sick and well, and it doesn't come with a road map or an instruction sheet.

When my treatment ended and the doctor said I was in full remission, I found myself in totally new territory. Expecting to feel happy and full of joy, instead I found myself feeling tense —and *lonely*. Now, *that* was an emotion I hadn't expected! But that's truly how I felt. Despite all my complaining about the ongoing tests and medications, and despite my weariness at the rigorous schedule of doctor appointments, when the oncologist announced that I would need only regular MRIs but not the weekly appointments I'd been hurrying off to for so long . . . it felt as though I were being tossed out on my own.

At first I didn't recognize the emotion that surged through my mind as days passed and I remained at home, not going anywhere; then awareness hit me. Even though Bill was right there with me. Even though my friends and family kept my phone ringing regularly, and the mailbox was always full, I felt very much alone.

REVEREND FUN WWW.REVERENDFUN.COM

HELLO, GOOD SIR, ARE YOU ON YOUR WAY TO SPEAK WITH GOD? PERHAPS YOU WOULD BE INTERESTED IN SOME 'GLORY BLOCKERS' SUNGLASSES ... IT GETS MIGHTY BRIGHT UP THERE.

Whenever loneliness oozes into our minds, it's easy for depression to set in, too, especially when medication-induced chemical changes are occurring within the body. And I fell victim to it; I experienced depression.

It took hard work, plenty of prayer, and help from my doctors and my friends to reset my attitude. Today I'm determined to see remission as a time of rebirth—a time of new life and hope. Indeed, I now see remission as an opportunity to gather my forces and learn a new identity. Now I'm a pioneer exploring new territory in this extended life God has given me.

So how do I cope while living on the edge? The simple little serenity prayer has been a great comfort to me during this time:

God, grant me the serenity
to accept the things I cannot change,
the courage to change the things I can,
and the wisdom to know the difference.

Cancer is a permanent part of my vocabulary now; I can't change the fact that I am a cancer patient—a cancer survivor. I accept that new classification, even though I don't like it. My attitude, however, is something I *can* change. Working hard to keep it on an upward track, I constantly pray for wisdom to realize when I need help.

Emerging, Changed, on the Other Side

While this book is about my cancer experience, I hope it has been helpful to anyone enduring difficulties. But for just a moment I want to speak directly to those who have been through cancer and come out the other side into remission. It's such a strange place! Of all the stages of my illness, it's the one that challenged me most.

For years I've said that openness is to wholeness as secrets are to sickness, and remission is a time for openness. If you're feeling anxious about the threat of the unknown, especially about fears that the cancer will return, talk to friends, family members, or professionals such as a minister or counselor

who can help you get the anxiety under control. Then let the feelings flow.

Don't be afraid you'll turn the person off. If you're meeting friends or family, set a time to get together and a time to leave, and hold to that schedule so both of you know your talk time *will* come to an end. If you do this, that person is more likely to be willing to meet with you as often as you need to. If the friend has come to your house, let him or her know you have something else scheduled to do at a specific time, and when that time comes, thank your friend for coming and gently guide him or her to the door. Bill and I tried to set time limits right from the beginning of the visit, mentioning that we had something scheduled at such and such a time and then gently ending the visit when that time came.

Support groups also can be of great assistance during this time of recovery and remission, because in those settings you realize others feel the same apprehension you do. You'll also see there is no right or wrong way to feel about what's happening to you. And you'll probably find that others feel the same way you do. The process of sharing with and listening to others in a group session will help validate your own feelings.

Try talking with friends, joining a support group, or working with a pastor or professional counselor. Find a way to cope with your emotions that works for you. And while you're finding listeners to talk to, make sure you include plenty of time talking with the Wonderful Counselor, too.[3]

As always during times of uncertainty, having accurate information is also essential so you don't get frightened by rumors. Instead of worrying about every little ache and twitch, ask your doctor: What symptoms should I watch for to know if the cancer has returned? What steps can I take to ensure a longer period of remission? Ask others who have been through similar situations for suggestions on how best to cope with day-to-day activities and concerns.

Having cancer move into remission is a powerful passage, and there are several ways to respond to that change. You can be fearful and full of worries. Or you can see it as a second chance to start life over, a time to set new priorities and seek out the things that are most important to your own well-being.

A Time of Grace and Blessing

Cancer and its treatment change you in many ways. You come out the other side different than you were before the diagnosis. But when you do come out of it, you can look at remission as a time of grace and blessing—a gift of time. Then the main challenge is to ask how you can use this gift well. Think about what you have learned from this ordeal. As one brain-tumor survivor wrote to me:

We never know what the Lord is trying to accomplish through us and in us. It would be nice to occasionally have a direct letter from God saying, "Barb, this is what I want you to do, learn, teach, etc." Oh, well, we'll just have to keep reading the letter He wrote to all of us!

Certainly, I have learned a lot during the last months. I've learned again that time is precious and life is short, and I don't take health and longevity for granted. I'm grateful for every breath!

And now, in this new stage of my life, I've learned that remission can enhance my life and bring peace to my soul. I've realized anew that peace comes through prayer, meditation, and sharing with others.

Have you heard about the trend among some churches to build labyrinths for Christians to walk through as a means of meditation and introspection? The ancient idea is being reborn around the country as churches lay down intricate pathways, usually bordered by stones or tape, that form a beautifully complex, round pattern. To those who don't know, it looks like a maze. But, as one church elder noted, there's a big difference. "A maze is designed to confuse and to trick," she said. "A labyrinth has one way in and one way out."[4]

The difference reminds me of what it must be like to face an illness like cancer—or any kind of crisis—as a Christian and as a nonbeliever. If you're a Christian, you see the convoluted pathway ahead of you and know there's a way out—the way that ultimately leads to heaven. Christians step onto that pathway full of faith and peace, knowing they will never be lost, understanding it as a place of growth and learning; they know that as they keep moving forward they will eventually come to the glorious end. Nonbelievers don't have that assurance. They see the same convoluted pathway, but not as a labyrinth in which they can grow in faith and hope. Instead they see a terrifying maze in which they can easily become lost forever.

Looking back from this position of respite at the end of the labyrinth, I believe there's been a purpose for the anxiety and stress I've endured. I can see how I've grown in faith, and I understand even more deeply the gift of grace God has given me. The experience reminds me of a picture I love. At first glance, it seems to be nothing but a hodgepodge of lines and blobs. But upon closer look, you realize it's the branch of a tree. The lines and streaks are limbs and leaves that are being blown by a harsh wind. And then you realize the form in the middle of the scene is a mother bird, her head bent into the storm, her body sheltering the eggs in her nest. In the midst of the storm, the scene is one of peace.

That's the message I hope to share in this book: peace in the midst of the storm. I want to extend a word of hope and a

message of faith to those walking the convoluted labyrinth behind me.

Remembering Our *Final* Outcome

No matter what passage we face—a step into remission, an end to some other problem we've confronted, or a plunge into the great unknown—we are assured that the final outcome will be worth whatever suffering we have to endure. In his book *A Bend in the Road*, David Jeremiah retells a story about a woman on a cruise ship with a large group of children. The ship, heading for New York, was caught in a ferocious storm in the middle of the Atlantic Ocean, sending many of the passengers into a panic. To calm the children, she gathered them around her and began telling them Bible stories. They soon became quiet, completely captivated by the wonderful stories.

Later, after the ship made it through the storm safely, the captain made his rounds. He had noticed earlier how the woman, talking and laughing with the children, had stayed calm throughout the storm.

"'How did you keep your cool when everyone else was falling to pieces?' he asked her. 'Have you been through something like this before?'

"'It's simple,' said the woman. 'I have two daughters. One of them lives in New York and the other one lives in heaven. I knew I would see one or the other of them in a few hours, and it didn't make any difference to me which one.'"[5]

With two sons in heaven and two sons here on earth, that woman's words could be mine. If surgery and chemotherapy and a daily muffin tin full of pills can keep cancer out of my life forever, hallelujah! I'll do my best to wring all the joy I can out of my remaining life on earth, cherishing my family and friends and appreciating each new sunrise. But if healing doesn't come, I'll be equally thrilled to hurdle the gates of heaven and throw my arms around my two sons who've been there for many years. Either way, I'll be happy. As the old hymn says, "It will be worth it all when we see Jesus."[6]

From *Why?* to *Whatever!*
Sometimes we pray long and hard, and then we wonder why God doesn't step in and calm the storm before it shipwrecks our lives. We wonder why He doesn't prevent terrorists from blowing up innocent people. We pray, as Jesus did, "Father, everything is possible for you. Take this cup from me,"[7] and yet the crisis comes anyway; the problem persists. Then too easily the *why?* of it all becomes our most persistent thought: *Why? Why? WHY?*

Forget *why!* However much you may scream that awful word at heaven, you will not get a satisfying answer. Instead, continue your prayer as Jesus did: "Yet not what I will, but what you will." In other words, "Whatever, Lord!" When you relinquish your life to God you'll find that He walks faithfully with you through the dark valley of suffering. He will redeem your pain and use it to bring you closer to Him.

ZIGGY   By Tom Wilson

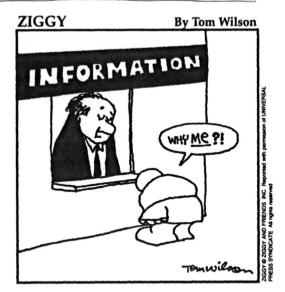

We have to get past the *why?* way of thinking and seek God's help in getting through the trial—and then be ready for the good that can come of it. Pain can purify and humanize the heart. Even deep loss, if we remain open to God's loving presence in our lives, can be redemptive and lead us into deeper compassion for others. God's glory can be revealed by His strength in us in all these trials. Our faith becomes perpetually stronger until it's fearless and unflinching. And in that steadfast position of faith, we are able to reach out to strengthen others. Albert Schweitzer once said that those who bear the mark of pain are never really free, for they owe a debt to those who still suffer.

Redeemed!

I love the word *redemptive,* and I love how God uses the struggles we face to redeem us and bring us closer to Him. Recently I was talking with a talented choir director who had been "outed" as being a homosexual and as a result he had to resign from his church. Now he has organized a new choir of several other guys who had also been misunderstood or had been cast out of their churches. Although it was hurtful to have his church reject him, he said the whole process of organizing the new choir to sing God's praises had been a redemptive one for him and these other young men.

The experience is perfectly expressed in the words of Fanny J. Crosby's beloved old hymn:

> *Redeemed—how I love to proclaim it!*
> *Redeemed by the blood of the Lamb;*
> *redeemed thru His infinite mercy—*
> *His child, and forever, I am.*
>
> *I think of my blessed Redeemer.*
> *I think of Him all the day long.*
> *I sing, for I cannot be silent;*
> *His love is the theme of my song.*
>
> *I know I shall see in His beauty*
> *the King in whose law I delight,*
> *who lovingly guardeth my footsteps*
> *and giveth me songs in the night.*

In the magnificent voices of these young men, lifted in loving admiration for God, beauty is made from something cast out.

Brokenness Brings Wholeness

Years ago I read a book, *Grace Grows Best in Winter,* by Margaret Clarkson, and it made such an impact on my life. Like the beautiful phrase that instantly encourages me in Fanny Crosby's hymn—"who . . . giveth me songs in the night"—the title of Ms. Clarkson's book instantly reminds me to watch for the blessings that can appear unexpectedly during any dark, painful ordeals I must face. She called the painful ordeals in which we find ourselves enclosed "God's hedges," and she described them this way:

> For those who believe in the love and wisdom of a sovereign God, who see His hand in all that concerns them, a God-hedged life, if a somewhat awesome, even a terrible thing, can be wonderful—a life of joy and freedom, a life of peace and praise, a life of thanksgiving and service.[8]

In so many ways, I've learned that even when I am hedged in by suffering and sorrow, the real beauty of my life comes out—like the sun reappearing from behind a dark cloud.

As someone said:

> God didn't promise us days without pain, laughter without sorrow, or sun without rain. But He did promise us strength for the day, comfort for the tears, and light for the way.

As we cling to God to get us through the dark times, our faith is strengthened until it becomes *unshakable.* That's another word I like, especially after having lived several decades here in Southern California earthquake country! It's also why I love that proclamation in Psalm 125:1: "Those who trust in the LORD are like Mount Zion, which cannot be shaken but endures forever." In our dark moments we can surrender ourselves into the hands of the One who will faithfully walk us through that time of trouble. We may never make sense out of the mystery of suffering, but we can participate actively in the healing process and entrust ourselves to the supreme source of love and wisdom.

Truly, we can advance much further in grace in one hour of suffering than in many carefree days of prosperity. Remember that grapes must be crushed to make the fine wine, and wheat must be crushed to make bread. Brokenness brings wholeness to all of us in a variety of ways. Broken hearts, broken bodies, broken dreams . . . and then, in the midst of our brokenness, we feel ourselves pressed against the unshakable presence of God. And there we find peace; there we find strength and courage for the next step.

If you have placed your trust in Jesus Christ, you can face calamity and crisis with hope. You can face cancer with courage. In His presence, you will find His wonderful grace for the next breath—and for the next day and the next. And even better, He will *use* your affliction for something good. He will bring you through it—in spiritual healing if the physical healing doesn't come. Either way, your faith will be stronger, and you will know you are redeemed forever.

Don't Rest in the Road Bumps
Some wise person said:

> Disappointments are like road bumps. They slow you down a little, but they also help you appreciate anew the smooth road afterward.

Isn't that the truth? And it reminds me of my foray into cancer and my emergence into remission. At first I was uncertain, but when I shifted my focus away from the obstacles and onto the big picture, life became much easier. In the same way, if you've driven over a rough section of highway or a potholed piece of roadway, you know the relief you feel when suddenly the pavement is smooth once more. If it hadn't been for the potholes, you probably would never have thought to appreciate just how smooth the ride was.

My life has followed the same kind of road. After spending those long, trying days in the hospital, I stepped outside and paused a moment, breathing in the fresh air, enjoying the beautiful blue sky and the songs of the birds. Surely the sky is never bluer and the bird songs never sweeter than they are when we step outside after a long period of confinement and appreciate anew this beautiful earth God has given us.

As I made that trip home from the hospital, it felt as if I had left behind a potholed section of roadway and was cruising onto smooth, new pavement. At that point the tumor was still in my brain and cancer was still threatening my health. But I had been given a second chance to enjoy whatever remaining time God chose to give me here. And I've been given several additional "second chances" since then, each time remembering that adage that says:

No one can go back and make a brand-new start, but anyone can start *now* and make a brand-new ending!

Leave the Screen Door Unlatched

Now, I know that sometimes we feel so low, we think we can't face another new day, can't climb back into the ring for yet another round of pain. Been there, done that! In the midst of suffering the deaths of my two sons and the estrangement of my homosexual son, I spent *months* cooped up in my bedroom, counting the roses on the wallpaper. But finally that moment came when I realized I could *choose* to be happy—whether or not happiness occurred spontaneously. I could make it happen.

That same attitude has carried me through the many ups and downs of my roller-coaster life ever since. When trials threaten to overwhelm me, I deliberately choose another way—God's way of boundless love, joy, and grace.

It's so easy, in the midst of painful times, to want to withdraw from life, shut the door, and turn off the phone. But that's the wrong thing to do—in so many ways. By shutting others out, we allow ourselves to be consumed by the problem. We also fail to share in the blessings that may come to *them* and to *us* as God works in all our lives.

A study by the Harvard Medical School found four attributes that are vital to "successful aging." (In my view, "successful aging" means surviving.) To pull yourself through whatever problem you're facing, grasp the hand of the Savior and strive to develop these outward-focused attributes in your life:

- Orientation toward the future. The ability to anticipate, to plan, and to hope.

- Gratitude, forgiveness, and optimism. We need to see the glass as half-full, not half-empty.

- Empathy. The ability to imagine the world as it seems to the other person.

- The ability to reach out. "We should want to do things *with* people, not do things *to* people or ruminate that they do things to us," says Dr. George E. Vaillant, director of the Harvard study. In other words, we need to "leave the screen door unlatched."[9]

awesome

Reach out. Live with an attitude of gratitude. And share yourself. Jesus directs us to invite others to share our Christian way of life—just as He invites us to share His. Recently I saw an article about the way Billy Graham has offered that invitation to so many thousands around the world. The article was reporting on Dr. Graham's Louisville crusade last year.

Slowed by age and illness, his voice was still strong and his message was still soul stirring, focusing as he often does on his "perennial themes of forgiveness, love, and unity," the newspaper reported. And then Billy Graham offered the invitation to that stadium full of listeners: "You may never have this opportunity again," he said. "This is a glorious moment that may never happen again in Louisville. You come. I don't care how far back you are. We will wait on you. You come. Come." And they came—10,700 of them.

The newspaper reporter was revisiting three of those thousands a few weeks later to see what had happened to them. This is what the writer found:

Their lives seem changed now, not in dramatic public ways, but inexorably, the way a tiny shift in navigation redirects a rocket to a different galaxy.[10]

That's what God's call can do—redirect us toward a different horizon, a different ending: heaven. I've heard His life-restoring voice calling me back to Him many times as life's storms and challenges have threatened to knock me off course. But in the dark times, God's invitation has persisted: "I don't care how far back you are. . . . You come. Come."

Won't you come, too?

Moments of Mirth in the Manure Pile

Buck O'Neil's words of wisdom:

Hug everybody you can. . . .
Drain the bitterness out of your heart.
Sing a little every day. . . .
Tell people you love them.
Listen to old people tell stories. They might
    teach you something.
Be there for old friends.
Always be on time. . . .
Hold hands with the person next to you.
    That way, they can't get away.
    And neither can you.[11]

Life is too precious to be picky,
Too brief to be bitter,
Too beautiful to be bored,
And too wonderful to be wasted.

—WILLIAM ARTHUR WARD

"Well, the doctors were right—they said I'd
be out of the hospital within a couple of weeks."

Heaven is not just pie in the sky by and by.
It's steak on the plate while you wait!

The perfect prayer for those of us prone to foot-in-mouth disease:

"Dear Lord, keep Your arm around my shoulder . . . and Your hand over my mouth!"

An exasperated mother whose son was always getting into mischief finally fumed one day, "Tommy, how do you expect to get into heaven, acting like that?"

Tommy answered, "Well, I'll just run in and out and in and out and keep slamming the door until Saint Peter says, 'For heaven's sake, Tommy, come in or stay out.'"

I asked God for water, He gave me an ocean.
I asked God for a flower, He gave me a garden.
I asked God for a tree, He gave me a forest.
I asked God for a friend, and He gave me you.[12]

If I knew it would be the last time I would see you fall asleep, I would tuck you in more tightly, thank the Lord for your precious life. I would watch you sleep for a while.

If I knew it would be the last time I would see you walk out the door, I would give you a kiss and a hug and call you back for one more.

If I knew it would be the last time I'd hear your voice, I would turn off the TV, put down the paper, and give you my full attention. I would remember the sound of your voice and the sparkle in your eye.

If I knew it would be the last time I heard you sing, I would sing with you and ask you to do it one more time.

If I knew it would be the last time I would be with you, I would want to make every moment count. I wouldn't worry about the dishes, the yard, or even the bills. If I knew it would be the last time, I would want to be with you all the time.

If I knew it would be the last time we were together, I would want to make you happy. I would cook your favorite dinner, play your favorite game. I would take the day off just to be with you. I wouldn't fuss so much about picking up toys and making the bed. I would remind you of how important you are to me. I would tell you how much I want you to go to heaven. I would tell you not to be afraid but to be strong. I would tell you that I love you, and with laughter we would share our favorite memories.

If I knew it would be the last time we spent together, I would read the Bible with you and say a prayer to God. I would thank the Lord for bringing us together and for taking such special care of us.

If I knew it would be the last time we were together, I would cry because I would want to spend more time with you.

If I knew it would be the last time . . .

I simply don't know when that time will be. Help me, Lord, to show my love to all the people who have touched my life. This may be the last time we are together.[13]

The first rule of survival:
Life ain't fair. Get used to it.

True!

Worry borrows. It's a disease of the future. It borrows the unknown trouble of tomorrow. The worrier loses the beautiful spirit of hope because worry paints such a gloomy, shocking, dreadful picture of the future.[14]

Better and sweeter than health, or friends, or money, or fame, or ease, or prosperity, is the adorable will of our God. It gilds the darkest hours with a divine halo and sheds brightest sunshine on the gloomiest paths. . . . I can assure you, . . . that you will find it the happiest place you have ever entered yet.[15]

Come now, you who say, "Today or tomorrow, we shall go to such and such a city, and spend a year there and engage in business and make a profit." Yet you do not know what your life will be like tomorrow. You are just a vapor that appears for a little while and then vanishes away. (James 4:13–14 NASB)

Acknowledgments

any thanks to all the friends who shared jokes, cartoons, and poems with me as I was recovering from cancer. Dozens of those rib-tickling items have been passed along in this book, to be shared with thousands of others. Thanks also to the writers of the encouraging letters and e-mails that came in as I was convalescing; many of those heart-touching messages are included here, too—with the writers' permission when we could track them down.

I'm also grateful to the artists who shared their wit in the dozens of funny cartoons that sprinkle these pages. Noel Ford of the United Kingdom was particularly thoughtful when, in lieu of a reprint fee, he asked that his payment be donated instead to the Red Cross Disaster Relief Fund.

Finally, I'm thankful for all the prayers on my behalf during the last year. At times, amid all the support of friends and Women of Faith attendees across the country, I felt as though I was nestling on a giant, prayer-filled pillow of love. Thank you, dear friends, for your love and your laughter. Both continue to be priceless treasures to me.

Notes

Chapter 1. I don't know what the problem is . . . but I'm sure it's hard to pronounce

1. Bern Williams, quoted in *Reader's Digest*, May 2000, 73.
2. Max Lucado, *Just Like Jesus*, quoted in *Grace for the Moment* (Nashville: J. Countryman, a division of Thomas Nelson, 2000), 19.
3. Paraphrased from Ron Gilbert, Ph.D., comp., *More of the Best of Bits & Pieces* (Fairfield, N.J.: Economics Press, 1997), 93.
4. Diane Crosby, quoted in Lowell D. Streiker, *Nelson's Big Book of Laughter* (Nashville: Thomas Nelson, 2000), 265.
5. *Uncle Duey's Proverbs, Book 2* (Apache Junction, Ariz.: Tract Evangelistic Crusade, n.d.), 5.
6. Arthur F. Lenehan, comp., *Best of Bits & Pieces* (Fairfield, N.J.: Economics Press, 1994).
7. Max Lucado, *When God Whispers Your Name* (Dallas: Word, 1994).

Chapter 2. Having a tumor . . . with humor

1. This poem was included in Mrs. Howard Taylor's book, *The Triumph of John and Betty Stam*, published in 1935 by China Inland Mission and re-released in 1982 as *John and Betty Stam: A Story of Triumph* by the Overseas Missionary Fellowship and is reprinted here with permission of OMF International. The footnote corresponding to the poem said, "This poem . . . concerns the noble steadfastness of the Rev. J. W. Vinson, martyred in North China, and was written by another China missionary, the Rev. E. H. Hamilton. This poem meant much to John [Stam]. He received it from Dr. C. E. Scott."
2. E. K. Bailey, quoted in Berta Delgado, "Now You'll Hear Me Preach with My Life," *Dallas Morning News*, 17 August 2001, 1.

3. Rob Gilbert, Ph.D., ed., *Bits & Pieces on HOPE* (Fairfield, N.J.: Economics Press, n.d.), 6.

Chapter 3. This would be funny if it weren't happening to *me*
1. Sylvia Wood, "Chemo: 'It's Not As Bad As You Think,'" *Albany Times Union*, quoted in the *Tampa Tribune*, 15 April 2001, Baylife 7.
2. Joshua 1:9.
3. Mark 16:17–18.
4. For information about the American Brain Tumor Association's pin, visit the Web site: www.abta.org or write to ABTA, 2720 River Road, Suite 146, Des Plaines, IL 60018.
5. Dr. David Jeremiah tells this story on an audiotape, "The Bend in the Road, Selected Scriptures," tape BIR01, of his *Turning Point* radio program. On the tape he describes his own struggle with cancer, and his insights have been fabulously encouraging to me. Bill and I have listened to that tape until we've almost worn it out. You can order a copy for $6 plus shipping by calling Turning Point at 800-947-1993.
6. William C. Poole, "Just When I Need Him Most," 1936.
7. Dave Weinbaum, quoted in *Reader's Digest*, February 2000, 69.
8. Original source unknown.
9. Source unknown.
10. Adapted from Harold Ivan Smith, *Decembered Grief* (Kansas City: Beacon Hill Press, 1999), 104.
11. Jewel, quoted in *Reader's Digest*, May 2001, 73.
12. Charlie "T." Jones & Bob Phillips, *Wit & Wisdom* (Eugene, Oreg.: Harvest House, 1977), 109.
13. Ibid.
14. *Bits & Pieces*, 15 July 1999, 11.

Chapter 4. I'm gonna laugh about this if it kills me
1. Ray Healey, Jr., "Take Two Jokes and Call Me in the Morning," *Strong Investor*, n.d., 8–9.
2. Ibid.
3. Lindsey Tanner, "Researchers Test Theory That Humor Hinders Pain," Associated Press story published in the *Wichita Eagle*, 2 September 2000.
4. Walt Duke, "Bob Dole to Bush: Keep Up the Laughter," *AARP Bulletin*, June 2001, 2.
5. See Psalm 30:11 and 45:7, 2 Corinthians 7:4, John 16:24, and Nehemiah 8:10.

6. Cynthia Kling, "O to Joy!" *O* magazine, May 2001, 104.

7. Study by University of Pennsylvania researcher Martin Seligman, cited by Claudia Smith Brinson, columnist for *The State* in Columbia, S.C., reprinted in the *Tampa Tribune*, 24 June 2001.

8. John 15:12.

9. John 15:11.

10. Frank T. Griswold, "May We Be Surprised by Joy this Lent," *Episcopal Life*, March 2001, 19.

11. See John 1:43–46.

12. Emilie Barnes, *My Cup Overflows with the Comfort of God's Love* (Eugene, Oreg.: Harvest House, 1998), 30–31.

13. Joyce Landorf, *Monday through Saturday* (Waco, Tex.: Word, 1984), 28–29.

14. Jeremiah 17:8 MSG.

15. John 6:68 NCV, emphasis added.

16. Joni Eareckson Tada, quoted in Ingrid Trobisch with Marlee Alex, *Keeper of the Springs* (Sisters, Oreg.: Multnomah, 1997).

17. 2 Corinthians 12 MSG.

18. Jill Scott, quoted in *O* magazine, May 2001, 213.

19. Joseph Barnby, "When Morning Gilds the Skies," 1868.

20. Valerie Monroe, "When You're Smiling . . . ," *O* magazine, May 2001, 183–4.

21. Pam Costain, "It's a Gift to Participate with Mom in the Process of Aging," *Minneapolis Star-Tribune*, 13 May 2001.

22. Henri J. M. Nouwen, quoted in *O* magazine, May 2001, 51.

23. "Survivor Cherishes Life after Ordeal," *South Florida Sun-Sentinel*, reprinted in the *St. Petersburg Times*, 14 August 2001, 3B.

24. Hannah Whitall Smith, *The Christian's Secret of a Happy Life* (Boston: G. K. Hall, 1973), 316, 325–6.

25. Adapted from Lowell D. Streiker, *An Encyclopedia of Humor* (Peabody, Mass.: Hendrickson Publishers, 1998), 241.

26. Ibid., 237.

Chapter 5. Give me ambiguity . . . or give me something else

1. See Matthew 27:32.

2. See 1 Corinthians 10:31, Colossians 3:17 and 3:23.

3. Proverbs 16:3.

4. Judges 6:14 TLB.

5. Judges 6:15.

6. Judges 6:14, 16.

7. Philippians 2:5–6 MSG.
8. Philippians 2:6–7, emphasis added.
9. "Secrets of a Life Well Lived—Lighten Your Load," *Reader's Digest*, April 2000, 99–100.
10. Ruth Bell Graham, *Footprints of a Pilgrim* (Nashville: W Publishing Group, 2001), 48–49.
11. Ernest Hooper, "A Few Worthy Causes to Chew Over," *St. Petersburg Times*, 5 September 2001, B1.
12. Landorf, *Monday through Saturday*, 43.
13. Matthew 6:3–4 MSG.
14. Matthew 25:21 KJV, emphasis added.
15. Richard Gillard, "Servant Song," © 1977 Scripture in Song, a division of Integrity Music, Inc. Reprinted with permission.
16. Anne Ezal letter in "Hints from Heloise" column, 16 August 2001, *Dallas Morning News*.
17. Poem excerpt used with permission of its author, Tammy Mercy.
18. Source unknown.
19. Original source unknown, adapted from "The Most Important People in Your Life," *Family Circle*, 1 November 2000, 5.
20. *Guidelines for Living*, 25 November 1993.
21. Stephanie J. Patterson, *Ah, to Be a Child Again!* (San Diego: Grossmont Press, n.d.).
22. Ibid.
23. Japanese proverb quoted in *Reader's Digest*, March 2000.
24. Streiker, *An Encyclopedia of Humor*, 159.
25. Kris Kristofferson, quoted by Tad Bartimus, "Promises from the heart," *Kansas City Star*, 18 February 2001.
26. Fred Rogers, quoted in Judith S. Gillies, "What's Important to Mister Rogers," a *Washington Post* article reprinted in the *South Bend* (Ind.) *Tribune*, 26 August 2001, E1.
27. Oprah Winfrey, quoted in Gilbert, *More of the Best of Bits & Pieces*, 75.
28. Gilbert, *More of the Best of Bits & Pieces*, 75.
29. Sir Philip Gibbs, quoted in *A Smile Increases Your Face Value* (Lombard, Ill.: Great Quotations, n.d.), 12.

Chapter 6. Just think: If it weren't for marriage, men would go through life thinking they had no faults at all
1. Vince Passaro, "As Good As It Gets," a review of Iris Krasnow's

book, *Surrendering to Marriage: Husbands, Wives, and Other Imperfections,* in *O* magazine, May 2001, 161.

2. Ibid.

3. Isaiah 1:18.

4. 1 John 1:9.

5. Bill Tammeus, *Kansas City Star* columnist, reprinted in the *Tampa Tribune,* 4 March 2001, 5.

6. Proverbs 28:13.

7. Sylvester Stallone, quoted in *Parade* magazine, 22 April 2001, 5.

8. Betty Schreyer and Kate Kelly, quoted in Janet K. Keeler, "Recipes for Life," *St. Petersburg Times,* 9 May 2001, D1.

9. Mark Wolf, "Sign Language," a review of John Gottman's book *The Relationship Cure* in the *Rocky Mountain News,* 7 July 2001, 2F.

10. *St. Petersburg Times,* 29 November 2000.

11. This story is from Luke 1:6–25, 57–64. The quotes and references used here are from *The Message.*

12. Submitted by Donna J. Lambert; original source unknown.

13. Jay Trachman, quoted in *Reader's Digest,* June 2000, 129.

14. Used with permission of Ken Rappleye.

15. Three wise women's comments adapted from www.pastornet.net.

Chapter 7. Everything is okay in the end. If it's not okay, then it's not the end!

1. See John 9:1–3.

2. 1 Peter 2:21.

3. Isaiah 9:6.

4. Raymond McCaffrey, "A Circle of Contemplation," *Washington Post,* 23 June 2001, B9.

5. David Jeremiah, *A Bend in the Road* (Nashville: Word, 2000), 14.

6. Esther K. Rusthoi, "When We See Christ," © 1941 by Singspiration.

7. Mark 14:36.

8. Margaret Clarkson, *Grace Grows Best in Winter* (Grand Rapids: Zondervan, 1972), 15.

9. Lou Ann Walker, "We Can Control How We Age," *Parade* magazine, 16 September 2001, 4.

10. Cathy Lynn Grossman, "Praise for the Crusader," *USA Today,* 15 August 2001, D1–2.

11. Buck O'Neil, quoted by Joe Posnanski, "Celebrate Life in the Year," *Kansas City Star* Forum section, undated clipping.

12. Source unknown.

13. Original source unknown; adapted by Roger Shouse and used with his permission.

14. Joyce Landorf, *The Fragrance of Beauty* (Wheaton, Ill.: Victor Books, 1979), 49.

15. Smith, *The Christian's Secret of a Happy Life*, 61.

For women only, this is one of Barbara's most unique books. With her zany collection of observations about "life between the Blue Lagoon and Golden Pond," Barbara jumps right in, showing women how to survive growing older with courage and joy.

Between the years of childbearing and grandparenting, a woman has a lot to juggle! Barbara Johnson shows how the road from marriage to menopause is filled with more than a few potholes . . . but provides women with more than enough hope and humor to make it through the journey.

Pack Up Your Gloomees is filled with bittersweet stories of Barbara's journey through the minefields of life and her wise and encouraging responses to letters from hurting parents. Each chapter ends with a laughter-packed collection of Gloomee Busters.

THOMAS NELSON
Since 1798

More joy from the
Geranium Lady!

God's Most Precious Jewels are Crystallized Tears contains the stories of twelve extraordinary women as they journeyed through incredible hardship to become sparkling jewels of joy and encouragement to others. Barbara includes her own story of grief turned to blessing with her signature touch of hope and humor. Woven throughout these inspiring stories are descriptions of real gemstones—their origin and their traditional meanings.

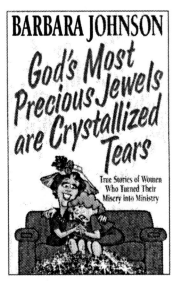

If you need a fresh breath of joy in your life, Barbara's 365-day devotional will help you look for life's little sparkles, even in the midst of life's most crippling sorrows. Love and hilarity bubble through these pages in equal doses as Barbara dispenses her unique blend of wisdom and zaniness to help thousands of hurting readers learn to laugh again. Each day's devotion features a Scripture passage and encouraging thought all wrapped up in Barbara's trademark style of offering firsthand advice about handling life's hardest hurts while dispensing infectious laughter and outrageous joy.

Bad news about your children carries a triple whammy of pain, worry, and "where did we go wrong?" Drawing on her own personal experience and the letters she has received from hundreds of hurting women, Barbara shares hope and humor to encourage parents in seemingly hopeless situations.

This is the book that started it all for the Geranium Lady! Sharing her own difficult experiences, Barbara proves that while pain is inevitable, misery is optional. If you need a fresh breath of joy in your life, this book is just the prescription for you. Barbara can help you look for joy, even in the midst of life's harshest challenges. This powerful book has sold one million copies and made Barbara a perennially best-selling author.

Barbara insists that laughing in the face of adversity is not a form of denial but a proven tool for managing stress, coping with pain, and maintaining hope. She zeroes in on the spiritual benefit of a smile, a giggle, and a good, old-fashioned belly laugh.

THOMAS NELSON
Since 1798

Barbara's approach to life is positive, uplifting, therapeutic and fun. *Splashes of Joy* offers an invigorating spurt of encouragement and a gentle reminder to splatter joy into the lives of others.

Sharing outrageous humor, rib-tickling insights, and inspiring, real-life examples, Barbara shows readers how to put life's trials into heavenly perspective. While we wait on Gabriel's horn to sound, Barbara gives women an external telescope with which to view their often difficult world.

THOMAS NELSON
Since 1798

This book has been enjoyed by and shared with: